BEGINNER'S BOOK OF
SAILING

BEGINNER'S BOOK OF

SAILING

Günther Grell

translated & adapted
by Barbara Webb

Henry Regnery Company · Chicago

Library of Congress Cataloging in Publication Data

Webb, Barbara, 1929–
    Beginner's book of sailing.

        Adaptation of Heut' geht es an Bord, by G. Grell.
    Includes index.
        1. Sailing. I. Grell, Günther, 1912–   Heut'
    geht es an Bord. II. Title.
    GV811.W35   1975   797.1'24   74-27808
    ISBN 0-8092-8292-5
    ISBN 0-8092-8238-0 pbk.

First published in Germany in 1968 with the title
Heut Geht es an Bord by Klasing & Co GmbH
© 1968 Klasing
First published in Great Britain 1972 by Ward Lock Ltd
in association with the Plume Press Ltd
This translation © 1972 Ward Lock Ltd
First published in the United States 1975 by Henry Regnery Company
        180 North Michigan Avenue, Chicago, Illinois 60601
Manufactured in the United States of America
Library of Congress Catalog Card Number: 74-27808
International Standard Book Number: 0-8092-8292-5 (cloth)
                                    0-8092-8238-0 (paper)

Contents

Introduction

When the wind starts to whistle around the corners, many people pull their hats down over their ears, put up their coat collars, and disappear rapidly into the shelter of the nearest doorway. But a man with even a spark of self-respect does not flee so abjectly from every fresh breeze; instead, he battles his way forward into the teeth of the wind and weather, responding to a primitive challenge to defy and master the elements, determined to be the hammer rather than the anvil. This is the stuff of which sailors are made—they are men who are not lightly deterred, who do not give up easily, but who are on intimate terms with wind, waves, weather, and storm.

Almost everywhere, even well inland, there is some stretch of water on which one can sail. Many a small boy has stood on the banks of a large or a small expanse of water near his home, racking his brains to figure out how he could learn to sail and be like Jim Hawkins or Sir Francis Drake.

One is almost ashamed to tell of the hours and effort spent in building a boat out of a few old planks, and in making a sail out of mother's old sheets, and then to tell how, when the splendid contraption was launched at last, it sank. This little play has been enacted time and time again, and not only by future captains, naval heroes, shipbuilders, and racing yachtsmen, for there is a drop or more of the sea in every man's blood. Not every boy who has pipe dreams of becoming a sailor finds his calling at sea, but these days it is possible for everybody to enjoy this splendid sport.

In a sailboat, agility is not all you need. By coming to terms with the wind and the waves, you acquire courage and endurance. Spending hour after hour tossed by the endless motion of the boat, perhaps concentrating at the helm with your mind and spirit stretched to the limit, and

then in addition having hard physical work to do—
manning the sheets and halyards, holding the main sheet,
and moving the tiller to and fro to keep the boat on
course—this is how a man finds his innermost self. But how
much easier it is to experience than it is to try to write about
it! On passage, the boat often meets with an unexpected
and unforeseen mishap when something breaks or pulls out;
then you have to set to and make repairs with the simple
tools and materials that are at hand.

This getting down to work and being self-reliant when
things are difficult is all part of seamanship. Sailing, after
all, is the school of seamanship, a school that is fun, where a
fresh breeze blows spray into your face, where the sun
shines, and where the splendid bellied sails move along like
the fleet of white clouds overhead. This seamanship, this
ability to be prepared and to take action, is not learned by
rote like Latin grammar, only to be forgotten. Seamanship
is useful throughout life and in every walk of life.

"Poor souls," cry the perpetual landlubbers, crossing
their fingers anxiously as they spot a tiny white sail far out
to sea, disappearing in the troughs of the waves when the
seas are high and the weather is foul. But the "poor souls"
out there are probably very happy and wish for nothing
better. And, in any case, what can go wrong if you are in
command of the situation and the ship is sound?

And next morning, when you reach some small harbor
after a stormy night, how quiet and still it is—no sudden
gusts, no tossing, just peace. Perhaps a few other boats
bobbing at anchor, an old gentleman ashore weeding his
garden, children playing; everything back to normal as if
nothing had happened—no storm, no sea so rough that you
had to battle your way forward inch by inch only a few
hours earlier. And then, isn't there a feeling of peace and
satisfaction when you relax with your wet clothes and sails
spread out to dry? That satisfaction will never be shared by
the "poor souls" on land who do not know the grandness of
the sea and sailing.

1
The Why and Wherefore of Sailing

The language of sail. Throughout this book, you will find new and strange words, often used to describe some rather common concepts and items of equipment. To the beginner, it may seem silly to learn this new vocabulary, but language is one of the most important tools of good seamanship. This language describes every piece of gear and every situation aboard a sailing vessel in terms that cannot be mistaken. Thus, when you find yourself in an emergency situation, you can call for a specific response (or be called upon by another sailor) in such a way that he immediately knows exactly what you are talking about.

Do not hesitate to learn this language and learn it well. The reason for it will become clear the first time you are in trouble. If you imagine all the ropes or lines aboard a sailboat, you will quickly understand the difference between the two expressions "Ease the jib sheet!" and "Let that rope go!" The term *jib sheet* tells you immediately what to do; the word *rope* is unclear. In the same way, all the unfamiliar words you will be asked to learn may well save you from an unfortunate and embarrassing dunking.

Wind. The wind plays the leading role when it comes to sailing. Two centuries ago great painters showed Boreas, the wind god, as an angel with a trumpet, his cheeks puffed out and his hands on his hips. When he is in a bad mood, Boreas stops blowing steadily, and instead plays all manner of tricks. By puffing more or less gently, or by moving his trumpet to one side or the other, he makes unpleasant and often dangerous gusts come whistling over the water from all points of the compass.

Wind force.   The strength of the wind can be measured according to a scale invented by Admiral Beaufort. In this country, most wind information is given and remembered in miles per hour. Most good sailors familiarize themselves with the Beaufort Scale, however, as it appears in much sailing literature. This scale, which is printed in full in Appendix 2, runs from force 0, calm, to force 12, hurricane. A yacht can reasonably expect to carry full sail at force 4, moderate breeze. When experts are around, it is as well for the beginner to claim that a strong wind was blowing one or two forces less than he thinks was the case, until he has learned by experience to estimate the force accurately.

Wind speed.   At sea, the speed of the wind is measured in knots (nautical miles per hour) or in meters per second; the wind forces thus have their speed equivalents in knots. For example, a twelve-knot breeze is the same as force 4, moderate breeze. You can estimate the speed of the wind in relation to the Beaufort Scale, but naturally you will need a little practice to do this, too.

Points of the compass.   On land, the four main or cardinal points of the compass—north, south, east, and west—are adequate for describing the wind direction, but this is not good enough at sea. The sailor divides his compass rose into 32 parts called points, each of which is 11¼°, making 360°

Fig. 1: The compass rose

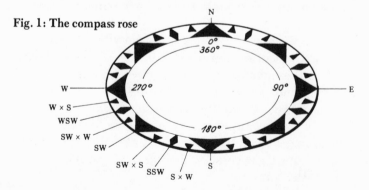

in all (Fig. 1). A right angle contains 8 points totaling 90°. For example, the sector from south to west consists of south, south by west, south-southwest, southwest by south, southwest, southwest by west, west-southwest and west by south. Points are usually written by abbreviating them to the initial letters, south-southwest being SSW. Today, however, since division of the compass rose into points becomes complicated (NW x W¾ W, for example) and can lead to mistakes, it is usually divided into degrees.

    Points can also be used to describe the direction of objects or marks from the boat (Fig. 2). If you are sailing

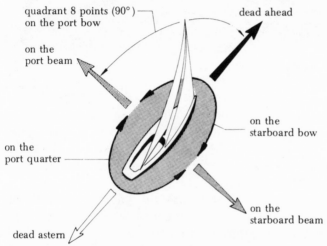

quadrant 8 points (90°)
on the port bow

dead ahead

on the
port beam

on the
starboard bow

on the
port quarter

on the
starboard beam

dead astern

Fig. 2: Directions from the boat

toward a buoy that is exactly over the bow, the bouy is said to be dead ahead; if it is to starboard (right) of the course, or to port (left), then it is on the starboard or port bow, and the angle between the object and the boat's course is described in points or degrees: "four points [or 45°] on the starboard bow." If an object is exactly at right angles to the boat, it is said to lie dead abeam to port or starboard.

Set of the sails.   From whichever point of the compass the wind blows, it is both friend and foe to the sailor, and his aim is always to make the best use of it. The wind blows onto a yacht from various directions (Fig. 3). If it comes

running   reaching   closehauled

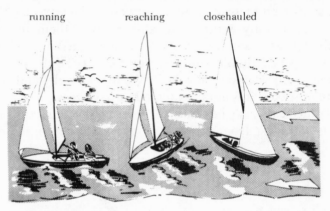

Fig. 3: Sailing points

from dead astern, the wind blows the boat away; she sails before the wind, running, with the sails set at right angles to the fore-and-aft line of the boat. Any old orange crate can sail downwind. It is possible to sail like this on land wearing roller skates and holding a cloak out on both sides like a sail.

If the wind blows onto the yacht in any direction between dead astern and abeam—in other words, to one side or the other but still abaft the beam—then the yacht is sailing with the wind free; she is broad-reaching. The sails will be set at an angle of between 85° and 45° to the fore-and-aft line of the boat. You can prove on land (on roller skates again) that the wind does push you forward even when it is not dead behind you. When the wind is abeam, a boat is on a beam reach, and when the wind is slightly forward of the beam, she is on a close reach.

The real skill in sailing is needed when the wind is blowing from ahead and at an acute angle to the boat. The sails then have to be hauled in almost parallel to the fore-and-aft line of the boat, which sails at an acute angle to the wind; she is on the wind, or closehauled, or beating. The better designed a yacht is, the closer to the wind will she sail. Racing yachts are the best at windward work.

It is possible to sail to a point that lies in the direction from which the wind is coming, but you cannot sail directly to it—you must zigzag to and fro (Figs. 4 and 5). This is

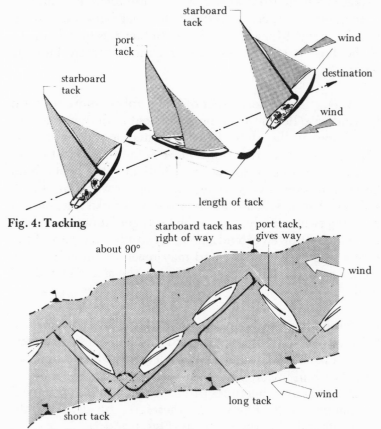

Fig. 4: Tacking

Fig. 5: Tacking in a narrow channel

called tacking, and the yacht works her way forward closehauled, first on one tack and then on the other, with sails alternately to port and to starboard. When you change the side from which the wind comes it is called tacking, coming about, or going about. When the boat is head-to-wind, she is said to be in stays if she is coming about, or in irons if she is making sternway and will not sail off on one tack or the other.

No one would be surprised to find that a boat can sail before the wind or with the wind free, but when the wind strikes the boat from ahead at an acute angle it would be reasonable to expect it to drive the boat backward, or at least to prevent forward progress. In fact this only happens if the boat is steered directly or almost directly into the wind.

The keel.   The whole secret of being able to move forward to windward lies in the shape of the boat underwater and in the shape of the sails. If you hoisted a sail on a flat-bottomed rowboat that floats more out of the water than in it, and then tried to sail her to windward, the boat would be driven sideways without moving forward at all. A sailboat does not float on top of the water like this; part of her underwater body, called the keel, goes down deep into the water. It often extends along a considerable part of the boat's length, is narrow, and may reach down only a few inches or several feet, depending on the size and type of boat.

Centerboard.   A dinghy does not have a keel, but instead has a centerboard or daggerboard that has the same effect. It is not part of the hull itself but is a plate or board that can be raised and lowered. Cruising boats that sail regularly in shoal waters are sometimes fitted with centerboards as well as shallow keels. Boats can, therefore, be divided into keelboats and centerboard boats (Figs. 6 and 7).

When the wind strikes the sails at an angle, it cannot drive the boat sideways because the keel or centerboard meets sideways resistance from the water. Because the keel prevents the boat from being blown sideways, the pressure of the wind on the sails makes her lean over; this is called

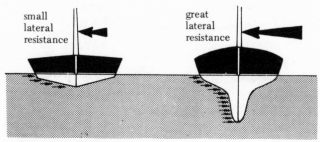

Fig. 6: **Dinghy and keelboat**

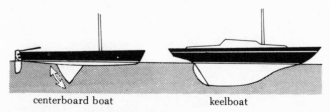

centerboard boat   keelboat

Fig. 7: **Centerboard boat and keelboat**

heeling. The wind cannot push the boat completely over, because the pressure of the wind on the sails above the water is opposed by the force of gravity on the weighted keel and by the buoyancy of the boat (Fig. 8). A boat is somewhat like one of those weighted toys that stands

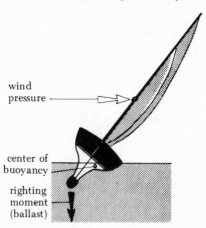

Fig. 8: **Noncapsizing keelboat**

straight up again as soon as you knock it over. As the pressure of wind on the sails eases, the boat returns to an even keel.

A centerboard does not weigh much and therefore cannot counteract so strong a wind. In gusty weather, if the pressure of the wind on the sails is not eased quickly enough by letting out the sheets, a dinghy will capsize (Fig. 9). This is not dangerous, because a dinghy filled with water floats.

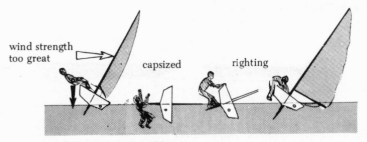

Fig. 9: Capsizing centerboard boat

Dinghies are light in weight and are constructed with built-in compartments that trap pockets of air or other methods of buoyancy so that they cannot sink. It is as well to ensure that buoyancy compartments really are airtight, and also that flotation materials are securely attached to the boat. After capsizing, it is essential not to leave the boat, for she will float and support the crew. She can easily be righted by standing on the centerboard while the jib and mainsail are left free to flap.

A keel yacht, in contrast, does not capsize, although she may be knocked down so far that the mast touches the water for a moment. The bottom of her keel is made of lead or iron and is so heavy that even in the worst of storms the strength of the wind does not cause her to capsize. If the wind and sea become too heavy, however, the mast and sails may go overboard. Boats can, therefore, also be divided into those that capsize (centerboard boats, Fig. 9) and those that do not (keelboats, Fig.8).

Because the boat cannot be driven sideways by the

wind, she will move in the direction where there is least resistance from the water—that is, forward. But why? A glider will stay up in the air and move forward because the wind streams over the upper and lower curved surfaces of the wings at different speeds, causing a vacuum on the upper surface that sucks the glider forward and upward. The same thing happens when sailing closehauled. The sails are not flat but made to curve (belly) so that they are the same shape as the wing of a glider; again, a vacuum is formed and sucks the boat forward. This effect can be greatly increased in racing yachts with a large jib called a genoa that reaches well aft, overlapping the mainsail and forming a wind funnel, a slot between the sails through which the wind streams more rapidly.

This "slot effect" belongs to the realm of aerodynamics—a realm that has by no means been completely explored as far as sailing is concerned. The causes of many things that the sailor, and above all the racing yachtsman, has learned from the observation of aerodynamic effects is not yet fully understood and remains rather a mystery.

windward   leeward

Fig. 10: Windward and leeward

Windward and leeward. Whether a yacht is running before the wind, reaching with the wind free, or closehauled, the wind blows onto one side of the boat and blows away from the other. The side onto which the wind blows first is the windward or weather side, and everything to that side of the boat is windward. The side toward which it blows and on which the sails normally lie, together with everything on that side of the boat, is leeward, pronounced "Loo-erd." Thus, the windward shore is the shore to windward of you, and the lee shore, onto which the wind blows, is to leeward of you (Fig. 10). When two boats are on the same body of water, the one nearer to the wind is the windward boat, and the other boat is to leeward of her.

2
About Shapes and Classes of Boats

A small floating plank can be pushed underwater quite easily with one hand. A bowl-shaped object of the same size is more difficult to sink, and two hands are needed to force it down into the water. Thus a bowl shape has greater buoyancy. (Have you ever seen empty shells floating in on the tide?) Every shape has different buoyancy characteristics. If you imagine a boat cut in half from side to side, you will see that a centerboard dinghy is U-shaped like a bowl, while a keel yacht is more V-shaped, like a wedge (Fig. 6). It takes a relatively strong wind to make a centerboard boat heel far over, because a hollow bowl is very buoyant. A much larger and more seaworthy keelboat will heel farther with less wind. Keel yachts, in fact, are so designed that they take the shape of a hollow bowl like a centerboard dinghy when they are heeled; their buoyancy increases, and they will not heel much farther than a certain point even when the pressure of wind on the sails is much greater.

There is great variety in the shapes of hulls. The forward end of the boat is the bow and the after end is the stern. It is primarily the shapes of bow and stern that give a boat her character, and they influence the lines of the hull. A boat designed for speed is usually long, for speed increases with length. The bow is drawn out and shaped rather like a

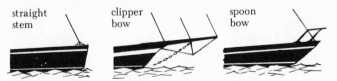

straight stem   clipper bow   spoon bow

Fig. 11: Shapes of bows

19

spoon (Fig. 11), while the stern is long, reaching over the water—a counter stern (Fig. 13). When a racing yacht like this heels over, the long, U-shaped bow and stern come into

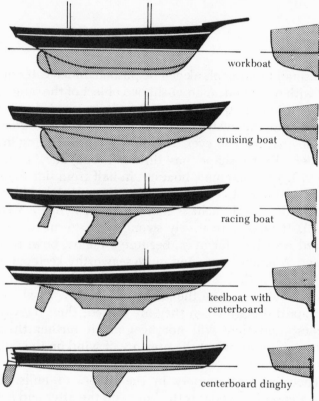

Fig. 12: Shapes of hulls

contact with the water, buoyancy is greatly increased, and she sails lightly over the waves at a much higher speed than if she were a simple wedge shape, plowing her way through the water and meeting great resistance. The naval architect who designs a yacht draws the shape of hull, bow, and stern according to whether she is to be a slender, rapid racing craft or a roomy cruising boat, and also according to whether she will be sailing in rough waters at sea or on smooth inland waters.

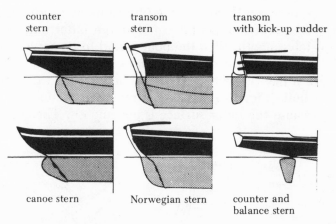

Fig. 13: Shapes of sterns

Parts of the hull. A wooden boat constructed in a traditional manner is built with a framework of numerous pieces of wood running both along and across the boat (Fig. 14), around which a solid shell—the planking—is fastened. This framework consists of the parts that run the length of the boat—the keel, stringers, and shelf. The transverse pieces are called frames, timbers, floors, and deck beams. If the planks are fastened close to each other on the ribs, and

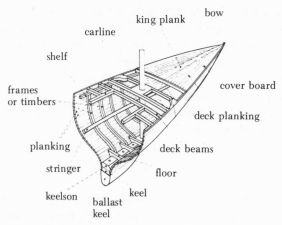

Fig. 14: Parts of the boat (forward)

the gaps between them are filled by caulking (with cotton and waterproof compound) so that the outer surface is completely smooth, then the boat is said to be carvel built (Fig. 15). If, however, each plank overlaps the plank beneath it like tiles on the roof of a house, then the boat is clinker built (Fig. 15). It is easy to recognize a clinker built boat because the outer surface is not smooth. The ends of

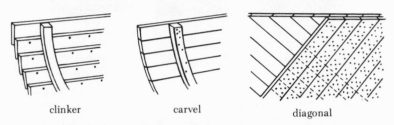

clinker   carvel   diagonal

Fig. 15: Types of planking

the planks are fastened to the stem forward, and either to the sternpost aft in the case of a canoe stern (Fig. 13), or to the transom in a boat with a counter or transom stern (Fig. 13). The stem and sternpost are strong and usually made of oak; they both are fastened to the keel.

The boat shown in Fig. 14 has a rounded-bilge. Her frames are curved, and she would have a rounded section if she were cut in half. A hard-chine boat is quite different (Fig. 6, left); her frames are straight, fastened to each other at an angle so that her sections are angular. The outer skin of both hard-chine and round-bilged boats can also be made of plywood, which results in a lighter boat. The hull is made up of layers of ply and is so strong in itself that a framework of ribs is unnecessary in the case of a small round-bilged boat. In addition to wood and plywood, boats are also made of fiberglass, steel, and aluminum.

Classes of yachts.   A man who sails for pleasure, often spending weeks alone or with just a few friends, dependent on his own resources and those of his boat, is really an individual. If each man were to have a boat built according to his own ideas and requirements, or if there were no classes, there would be designs without number, all different from each other. Since the advent of fiberglass construction, a large number of boats is often made from the same mold. This method of production not only keeps the price down but results in "families" of sister ships called classes. Classes may also consist of boats built according to regulations laid down by various racing organizations to make possible fair and even competition among boats.

Racing classes.   Racing classes are governed by many rules as to length of hull, beam (breadth), draft (depth), equipment, type and size of sails, and so on.

International classes are those recognized by the International Yacht Racing Union, the IYRU, whereas regulations for North American classes are the concern of the North American Yacht Racing Union, the NAYRU. There are keelboat classes and centerboard classes, and both may be either restricted or one-design. In restricted classes the rules are so drafted that designers have some freedom, and boats that do not look alike are developed for the same class. For example, some classes are restricted solely on the area of their sails when closehauled, while the hull is in no way restricted. The result is great variation in hull shape. One-design boats, in contrast, are all built to exactly the same plan; they are first and foremost racing yachts, designed for competition among exactly similar boats. In racing a one-design boat, it is only the skill of the helmsman and crew that counts, not the arts of the naval architect.

Fig. 16: International one-design and restricted classes

International
5.5 meter class

International
Dragon

International
Star

International Soling

Flying Dutchman

International
Finn

Tempest

5.5 International 5.5-meter restricted class. Keelboat. Sail markings: 5.5 with national letter and number of boat. Length overall about 9–10 m.; length waterline about 6.50–6.90 m.; minimum breadth 1.90 m.; maximum draft 1.35 m.; sail area 26–28 m².; displacement from about 1.8 tons. No self-draining cockpit. Crew: 3.

D   International Dragon one-design Class, designed by J. Anker, Norway. Keelboat. Sail markings: D with national letter and number of boat. Length overall 8.90 m.; length waterline 5.70 m.; beam 1.90 m.; draft 1.20 m.; displacement 2 tons; sail area 20 m². No self-draining cockpit. Crew: 3.

★   International Star one-design class. Hard-chine, with keel and balanced rudder. Sail markings: a five-pointed star with the number of the boat. Length overall 6.90 m.; length waterline 4.80 m.; beam 1.70 m.; draft 1 m.; sail area 26 m². No buoyancy compartments. Crew: 2.

Ω   International Soling one-design class, designed by Jan H. Linge. Keelboat with balanced rudder. Sail marking: an omega with national letter and number of boat. Length overall 8.15 m.; length waterline 6.10 m.; beam 1.90 m.; draft 1.30 m.; displacement 1015 kg.; sail area 21.7 m². Buoyancy compartments. Crew: 3.

FD   International Flying Dutchman one-design class. Centerboard boat, trapeze. Sail markings: FD with national letter and number of boat. Length overall 6.05 m.; beam 1.80 m.; weight 170 kg.; draft with centerboard 1.10 m.; sail area 15 m². Crew: 2.

≈   International Finn one-design class, designed by Richard Sarby, Finland. Una-rigged. Sail markings: 2 waves with national letter and number of boat. Length overall 4.30 m.; length waterline 4.23 m.; beam 1.40 m.; weight 100 kg.; sail area 10 m². Crew: 1.

T   International Tempest one-design class with retractable bulb keel, designed by Ian Proctor. Length overall 6.69 m.; beam 1.96 m.; draft 1.10 m.; weight 426 kg.; sail area 22.9 m². Crew: 2.

Fig. 17: Various racing classes

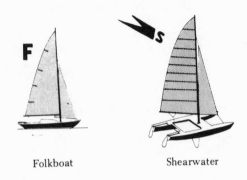

Folkboat   Shearwater

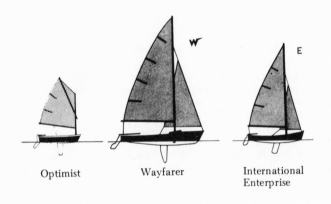

Optimist   Wayfarer   International
Enterprise

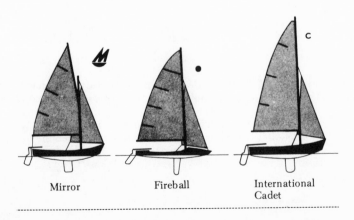

Mirror   Fireball   International
Cadet

F   Folkboat. A cruising boat widely sailed in Europe. Clinker or carvel construction. Sail markings: F and number of boat, sometimes with national letter. Length overall 7.66 m.; waterline length 6 m.; maximum beam 2.20 m.; draft 1.20 m.; displacement 2.15 tons; sail area 24 m². Crew: 3.

S   Shearwater III one-design catamaran. Plywood of fiberglass. Length overall 5.03 m.; beam 2.30 m.; draft with centerboard 0.78 m.; weight 163 kg.; sail area 14.86 m². Crew: 2.

Optimist. Plywood children's dinghy. Length overall 2.31 m.; beam 1.13 m.; draft with centerboard 0.77 m.; minimum weight 55 kg.; sail area 3.30 m².

W   Wayfarer one-design racing or cruising dinghy. Length overall 4.82 m.; beam 1.85 m.; draft 1.16 m.; weight 165 kg.; sail area 13.10 m² or 11.61 m² (cruising). Crew: 2.

E   International Enterprise. Wood or fiberglass. Length overall 4.03 m.; beam 1.60 m.; draft 0.98 m.; hull weight 90.72 kg.; sail area 10.48 m² or 7.43 m² (cruising). Crew: 2.

M   Mirror. One-design plywood dinghy. Length overall 3.30 m.; beam 1.4 m.; draft with centerboard 0.76 m.; sail area 6.4 m²; weight 61 kg. Crew: 2.

•   Fireball one-design racing dinghy. Length overall 4.93 m.; beam 1.41 m.; weight stripped 75 kg.; sail area 11.42 m². Crew: 2.

C   International Cadet. One-design plywood dinghy. Length overall 3.22 m.; beam 1.27 m.; draft 1.07 m.; weight 54 kg.; sail area 4.16 m². Crew: 2—under 18 years only.

Handicap classes.   Yachts that are not built to any particular rule can race against each other in handicap races. The difference between the boats is canceled out by an allowance based on a handicap formula that aims to give an equal chance of winning to boats of different sizes, speed, and so on.

Nautical language includes quite a few other terms that refer to kinds of boats. A cruiser is a keelboat with a cabin in which the crew can live aboard. Twin-keel boats, which are mostly used in shoal waters, do not have one deep central keel but two that together weigh the same as a normal keel but draw less (are not so deep). They are fixed on either side of the centerline of the boat at an angle at the turn of the bilge. Multihull boats have more than one hull; a catamaran has two and a trimaran has three.

3
Nautical Language

Nautical language is nothing more or less than the language of the sea and is as old as the sea itself. It is clear, precise, and to the point. A landlubber aboard will indeed find himself at sea when it comes to listening to instructions aboard unless he has some knowledge of the names of parts of the boat and some understanding of what the orders given mean. "Cast off the painter" brings visions of a man swimming furiously with a paintbrush between his teeth, but it means to untie the rope, or line, by which the dinghy is attached to the boat. The gooseneck is not to be wrung, but is the fitting that connects the boom to the mast. A sheet is not a vast expanse of cloth, but the rope that controls it. The list of words that are the same as those used daily on land but that have entirely different meanings on board is never-ending, and the beginner will do well to keep alert and make a mental note of the pitfalls.

Two words must be known before setting foot aboard: port and starboard. Originally the words were starboard and larboard, but *port* superseded *larboard* as less likely to be confusing. *Starboard* stems from the earliest days of sail, when a boat was steered by a plank or board fastened to the right-hand side of the vessel, which was therefore known as the steerboard side. The starboard side is the right-hand side of the boat when looking forward.

In contrast to the windward and leeward sides of the boat, which change depending on the direction from which the wind is blowing (Fig. 10), port and starboard never change.

A boat on starboard tack (Fig. 4) is one that carries her boom to port because the wind is on her starboard side. The

International Regulations for Prevention of Collision at Sea and the Racing Rules give priority to the boat on starboard tack, which has right of way over the port-tack boat. The starboard side of the boat is generally considered to be the more important.

The word *knot* as applied to the speed of a boat is often misused by landlubbers. A knot is a nautical mile per hour, so you speak of a boat sailing at five knots, which means that she is sailing at five nautical miles per hour. (You do *not* say that she is sailing at five knots per hour.)

The influence of nautical language on everyday speech is far-reaching and fascinating. Phrases such as "between the devil and the deep blue sea" or "the devil to pay" refer to the outboard plank, or devil, on the top deck—always the most awkward one to caulk ("pay") when making the deck watertight. The "bitter end" is the end of the anchor chain that is made fast below deck so that anchor and chain will not be lost overboard. In the old square-riggers it was made fast to bitts and was therefore called the *bitter* end of the chain. There are many more: "cut and run" refers to a situation in which the bitter end is cut so that the boat can run for shelter in an emergency; "the coast is clear" means that there are no underwater dangers; "swinging the lead" is the easy way out when sounding (determining the water's depth) by swinging the lead underarm instead of overarm; "taken aback" refers to the jib when the wind catches it on the wrong side quite unexpectedly (and usually most inconveniently), leaving the boat in irons and drifting backward.

There is a lot to learn and to the beginner it may seem easier to "tie up the rope that pulls up the big sail" rather than to "cleat the main halyard," but on a boat one has little room or time for mistakes and misunderstandings, so orders must be clearly and precisely given and understood.

4
The Rig

It is the sails that bring a boat to life. They can be made out of light or heavy material depending on whether they are intended for light or heavy weather. Cotton or, more usually today, a synthetic material is used. Narrow strips of material called cloths are sewn together, and the whole sail is bound with rope called the bolt rope. The edges of triangular sails are called the luff, leech, and foot (Figs. 18 and 19). Frequently the luff of a headsail has a wire sewn inside the seam instead of a stretchy bolt rope. The leech is considerably curved, and the area between the leech and a straight line from head to clew is called the roach.

In heavy weather the sail area is reduced by reefing. As shown in Fig. 18, reef points are sewn along the sail and cringles sewn into the sail in both the luff and the leech. First the luff cringle is brought down and made fast to the boom, then the leech cringle; finally the reef points are tied, with reef knots, around the sail but not around the boom. When shaking out a reef, the reverse order is used: first reef points, then the leech, and finally the luff. Another method of reefing is roller reefing—rolling the sail around the boom by rotating the boom; this method is quicker but has disadvantages in that the sail does not set so well and must be fully hoisted before being roller reefed. Modern offshore racing boats generally use a system of cringles and line left permanently set in the sails and called jiffy reefing.

It is very often easier to reef a sail if the boat is hove to with the jib aback, the mainsail in, and the helm lashed to leeward; the boat will then sail slowly forward, moving quietly with the waves.

Fig. 18: The mainsail

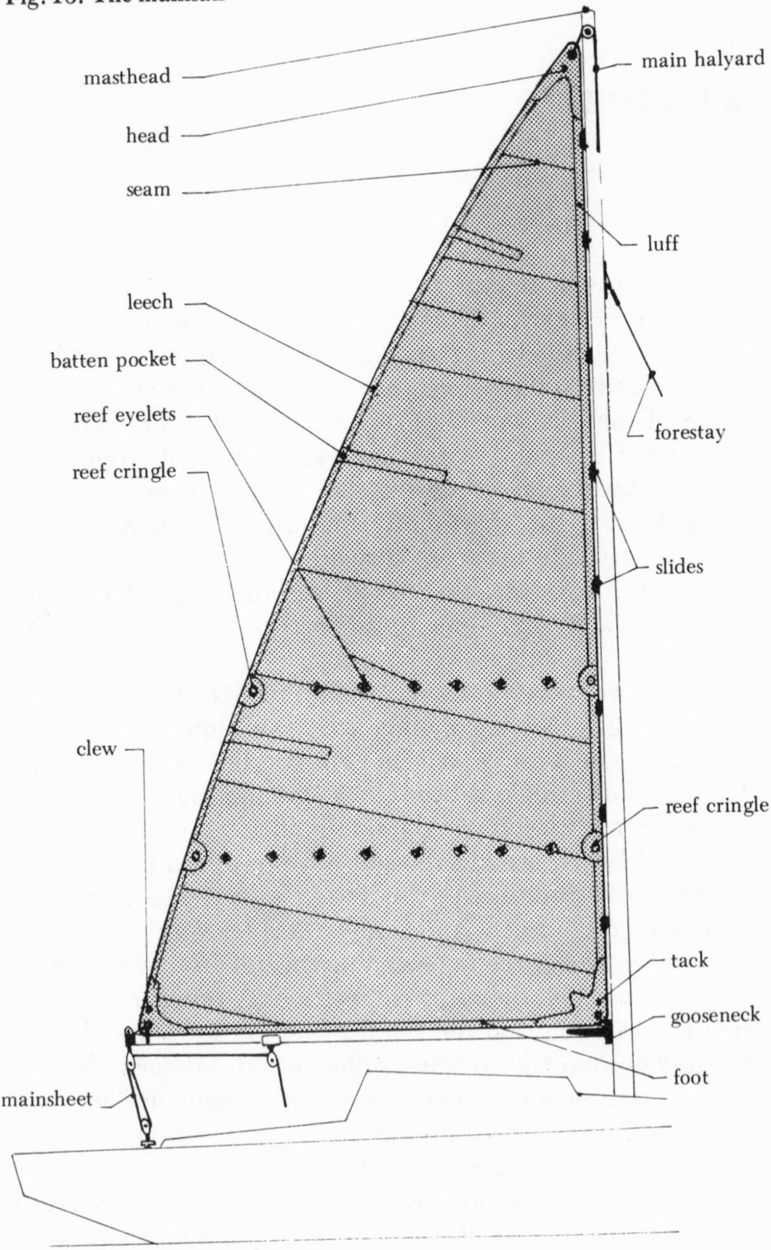

masthead

head

seam

leech

batten pocket

reef eyelets

reef cringle

clew

mainsheet

main halyard

luff

forestay

slides

reef cringle

tack

gooseneck

foot

Fig. 19: The jib

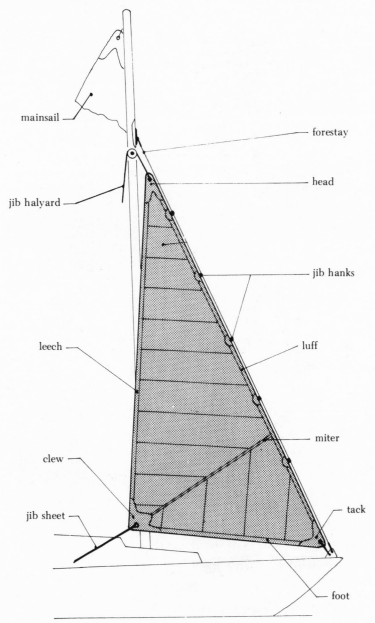

mainsail

jib halyard

leech

clew

jib sheet

forestay

head

jib hanks

luff

miter

tack

foot

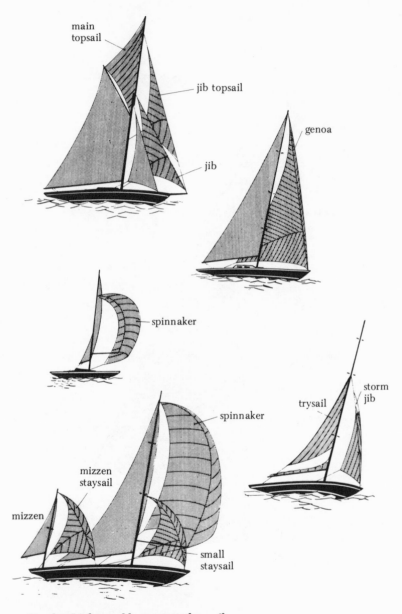

Fig. 20: Light- and heavy-weather sails

Types of sail.   Working sails are those that can be carried in a fresh breeze. They are the basic sails of a boat: the mainsail, which is hoisted on the mast; the headsail or headsails, which are set before the mast; and, in two-masted boats, the mizzen. Light-weather sails (Fig. 20) are carried in addition to or instead of working sails. Examples are the genoa, the topsail, and the spinnaker. Heavy-weather sails, which replace mainsail or working jib, are the trysail and storm jib (Fig. 20). Staysails are triangular and are so called because their luffs run parallel to a stay (a wire running up at an angle to the mast, which it supports). Mainsail and mizzen are usually triangular Bermuda or Marconi sails, but their luffs run vertically up a mast. There are also quadrilateral or four-sided mainsails and mizzens called gaff sails; the gaff is a spar to which the head of the sail is lashed. The sails, the spars, the standing rigging, and the running rigging together make up the rig.

The spars.   Fixed spars are the mast(s), the bowsprit, and the boomkin. The bowsprit extends forward of the bow and the boomkin aft of the stern as in the Bermuda yawl in Fig. 27. The very top of the mast is the truck; the bottom is the heel, which fits into the mast step. The hounds are where the standing rigging is attached to the mast.

Standing rigging.   Standing rigging is usually wire, and it supports the fixed spars. Stays support in a fore-and-aft direction: headstay, jumper stays, backstay (Fig. 21), and the bobstay under the bowsprit. Shrouds give support in an athwartships direction and are held out by the crosstrees or spreaders; there are three kinds: lower shrouds, upper shrouds, and diamond shrouds. The running backstays (Fig. 21), which support the mast aft at an angle, are part of the standing rigging although they are not permanently fixed; in order to let the mainsail out, one or the other running backstay has to be released.

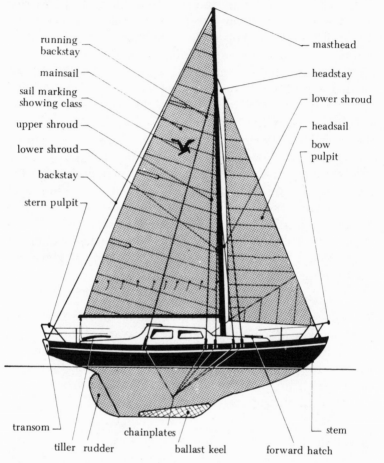

running backstay

mainsail

sail marking showing class

upper shroud

lower shroud

backstay

stern pulpit

masthead

headstay

lower shroud

headsail

bow pulpit

transom

tiller   rudder

chainplates

ballast keel

stem

forward hatch

Fig. 21: A yacht

Running rigging.   Running rigging is all the moving parts of a vessel's rigging, those lines and wires that run through blocks, thimbles, or eyes, and that constantly need to be adjusted—that is to say, all lines that are manned. The only exception is the running backstays, which run through blocks and are manned, but, as they support the mast, are part of the standing rigging. The trim of the sails is adjusted by hauling in or letting out the sheets, which are lines named after the sails to which they are attached: jib sheet, main sheet, and so on. The spinnaker sheet (Fig. 20) is attached to the spinnaker clew, which blows out to leeward, and the spinnaker guy hauls the spinnaker boom or spinnaker pole aft. The halyards, so called because they originally hauled the yards up the mast of a square-rigger, are also named after the sails they serve: spinnaker halyard, main halyard, and so on. Halyards and sheets that hoist or trim heavy sails often pass through several blocks in order to reduce the effort needed to work them: this is called a tackle. Winches usually are used to tighten sheets and halyards in larger boats (Fig. 24). Sheets and halyards generally are made fast to cleats (Fig. 25). Racing boats often use jam cleats for speedy working. Blocks, lines, and wire ropes are connected to each other and to the sails by shackles (Fig. 22).

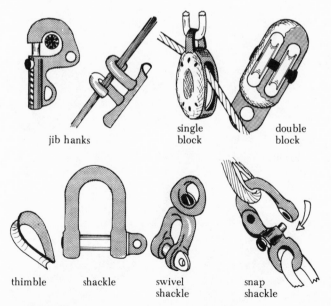

jib hanks   single   double
                   block   block

thimble   shackle   swivel   snap
                      shackle   shackle

Fig. 22: Fittings

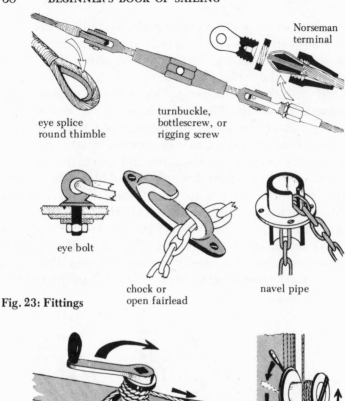

Norseman terminal

eye splice
round thimble

turnbuckle,
bottlescrew, or
rigging screw

eye bolt

chock or
open fairlead

navel pipe

Fig. 23: Fittings

sheet winch

halyard winch ·

Fig. 24: Fittings

Fig. 25: Making fast to a cleat

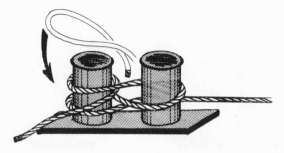

Fig. 26: Making fast to bitts

Types of rig. Sailboats are described according to the number of their masts and the arrangement and shape of their sails (Figs. 27, 28, and 29). Fore-and-aft mainsails are either four-sided gaff sails or the more modern triangular Bermuda or Marconi sails. A sloop has only one mast and carries a mainsail and headsail; she can be either gaff- or Bermuda-rigged. A cutter has two sails forward of her single mast and usually a bowsprit. A schooner has two or more masts, the mainmast being as high as or higher than the foremast. In ketches and yawls the mizzenmast aft is lower than the mainmast forward. The yawl has a small mizzen, and the mizzenmast is usually stepped aft of the rudder, while the ketch has a larger mizzen, and her mizzenmast is stepped forward of the rudder. The sails used in times past and rarely seen today, which hang down from spars called yards at right angles to the masts, are called square sails, and a vessel with such sails is square-rigged as opposed to fore-and-aft-rigged.

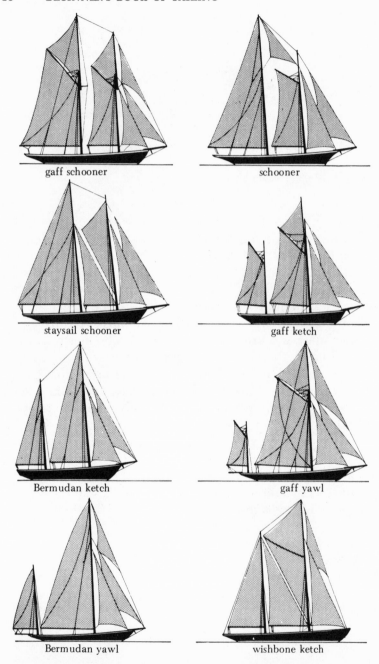

gaff schooner

schooner

staysail schooner

gaff ketch

Bermudan ketch

gaff yawl

Bermudan yawl

wishbone ketch

Fig. 27

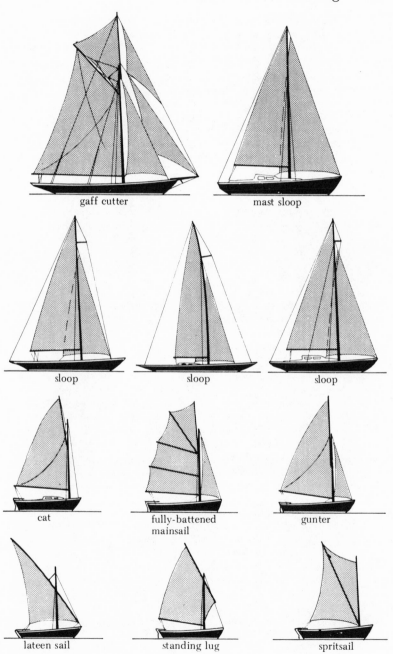

gaff cutter

mast sloop

sloop

sloop

sloop

cat

fully-battened
mainsail

gunter

lateen sail

standing lug

spritsail

Fig. 28

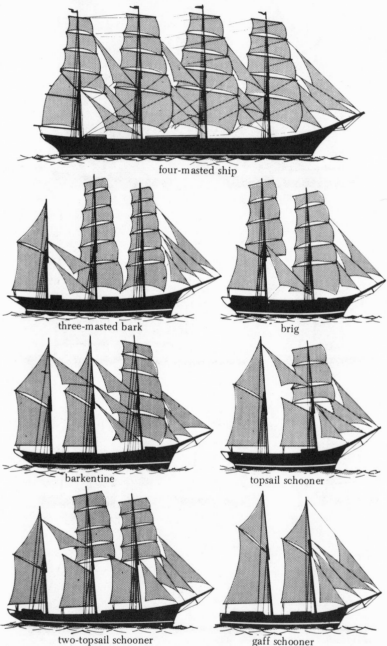

four-masted ship

three-masted bark

brig

barkentine

topsail schooner

two-topsail schooner

gaff schooner

Fig. 29

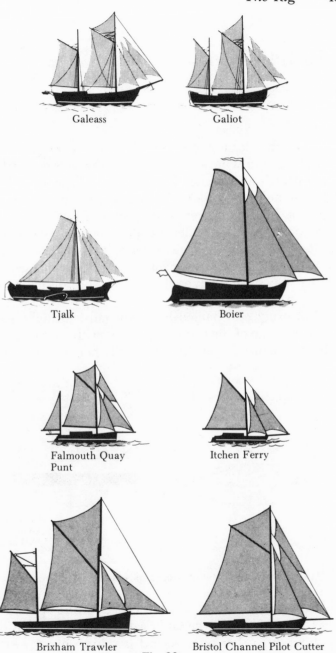

Galeass

Galiot

Tjalk

Boier

Falmouth Quay
Punt

Itchen Ferry

Brixham Trawler

Bristol Channel Pilot Cutter

Fig. 30

5
A Little Theory

Even the glossiest and thickest books cannot teach you to sail a boat to windward or to trim the sails correctly. A sailing boat is alive—each boat has her own special whims and idiosyncrasies, which you must get to know if you are to get the best out of her on all points of sailing. You can notice how alive and independent a boat is, especially at sea, for you cannot hold the tiller or the wheel absolutely steady, but must let it move a little so that the boat can find her own way as she rises easily to a crest or falls to a trough in the waves.

Not every closehauled boat will sail a straight course when you let go of the helm for a moment. If she does, she is perfectly balanced (Fig. 31). Normally her bow will move

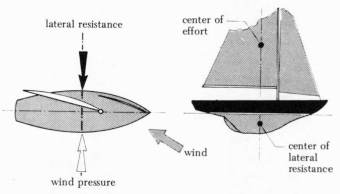

Fig. 31: CE and CLR (center of effort and center of lateral resistance)

either toward the wind, which is called luffing up, or away from the wind, which the sailor calls bearing away. A boat that luffs up of her own accord is said to carry weather helm, while a boat that bears away carries lee helm (Fig. 32). Why this happens and how it can be remedied is easily explained in the case of a boat with one mast.

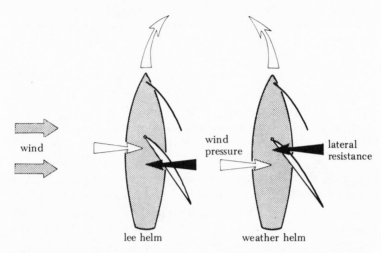

wind

wind pressure

lateral resistance

lee helm   weather helm

Fig. 32: Weather and lee helm

Center of lateral resistance.   Every ship turns around an axis, like the rod in the middle of a globe or a spinning top. The bottom end of this axis is called the center of lateral resistance (CLR). It is the central point around which the hull of the boat turns and is approximately in the center of the keel. It is obvious that a boat will pivot about the center of a long, narrow surface that extends deep into the water. If, however, a large amount of ballast is stowed aft so that the stern no longer floats on the water but dips beneath it while the bow is correspondingly lifted out of the water, then the shape of the hull beneath the surface is entirely altered, and the CLR will no longer be in the center where the designer intended but will have wandered farther aft. The boat is no longer well balanced and will not turn so easily around this new center.

Center of effort of the sails.   The sails also have a center, which is the upper end of the axis. This is called the center of effort (CE) and is usually just aft of the mast in the mainsail. If you imagine a boat pivoting about the mast, you can easily see that if the same amount of wind blows onto the sails forward of the mast as on the sails aft of the mast, the scales are evenly balanced and the boat will not tend to turn. If the size of the jib is increased, there will be more wind pressure forward of the mast; the bow will be weighed down; and the boat will bear away from the wind. The same thing happens if the mainsail is let out so that there is no wind pressure on it—the continuing pressure of the wind on the sheeted jib will push the bow to leeward. Conversely, if the mainsail size is increased or the jib left flapping, then the pressure of the wind will be greater aft of the mast, pushing the stern away and causing her to luff up toward the wind. This is exactly what occurs when tacking, after the jib sheet is cast off. Normally the CE of the sails lies almost perpendicularly over the CLR but slightly forward of it; the line between the CE and the CLR is the axis around which the ship turns.

It is a good thing to think over the ways a boat will react to sail adjustment before and abaft the mast and then to experiment, so that in any critical situation you can react correctly at lightning speed. The importance of understanding the relationship between the set of the sails and the course is shown by the fact that it is possible to steer without the rudder at all just by using the sails if, for example, the rudder is broken. Again, you can help the rudder in a boat that is slow to come about by backing the

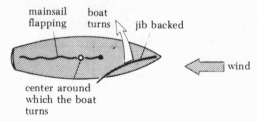

Fig. 33: Backing the jib

jib, sheeting it to windward and thus forcing the bow around (Fig. 33). When leaving a mooring, too, since the rudder has no effect until a boat is moving through the water, you can turn her in the right direction by backing the jib.

Briefly then:

> To bear away—slack off the main sheet and keep the jib drawing.
> To luff up—keep the mainsail full and let the jib sheet fly.

Lee helm.   Lee helm can be increased (or weather helm reduced) by:

> Increasing the size of the headsail
> Setting the headsail farther forward
> Bending or raking the mast farther forward by adjusting the stays
> Stepping the mast farther forward
> Reducing the size of the mainsail
> Stowing movable ballast farther aft
> Raising the centerboard and rudder on centerboard boats

Weather helm.   Weather helm can be increased (or lee helm reduced) by:

> Reducing the size of the headsail
> Setting the headsail farther aft
> Raking the mast farther aft
> Increasing the size of the mainsail
> Stowing movable ballast farther forward

Alterations like these to the rig or to the submerged surface of the hull to correct lee or weather helm may be necessary in order to get a nicely tuned and balanced boat.

6
Maneuvering under Sail

Steering. Most medium-sized and small yachts are steered by a tiller that is fastened to the rudder post. When the tiller is moved to port, the rudder moves to starboard, causing the bow of the boat to turn to starboard. As the wind is always the most important factor in sailing, alterations in course are referred to in relation to the wind. When the boat bears away from the wind, the bow turns away from it; when she luffs up, the bow turns up toward the wind. In order to make a boat bear away, you must move the tiller toward the wind. Because the windward side of a heeling boat is higher than the leeward side, you put the helm *up* in order to bear away. Likewise, you put the helm *down* toward the water, away from the wind, in order to luff up.

new course,
closehauled

haul in
sheets
(boat turns toward
the wind)

old course,
reaching

Fig. 34: Luffing up

Coming about. When the boat comes about or tacks (Fig. 35) she turns toward the wind so that her bow passes

48

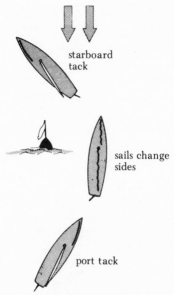

starboard
tack

sails change
sides

port tack

Fig. 35: Coming about

through the eye of the wind, and the sails move from one
side of the boat to the other. The helm is put down and the
boat luffed hard until the sails and bow are dead into the
wind. The helm is kept down, and she then falls away onto
the new tack. A large boat that carries a lot of way, or one
that is very maneuverable, can be tacked slowly, gaining
distance to windward while shooting up toward the wind.
But a boat that tacks unwillingly or one that loses way
easily, such as a centerboard boat, must be tacked quickly.
On the command "ready about," the leeward jib sheet is
uncleated and held fast ready to be released. As he says
"hard alee," or "helm's alee," the helmsman puts down the
tiller, the lee jib sheet is let fly, and, once the bow has
passed through the eye of the wind, the old weather jib
sheet, which now becomes the lee jib sheet, is hauled in and
made fast. Should the order "back the jib" be given (Fig.
33), the jib sheet should not be let fly, or if it is free, it
should be hauled in hard again. The wind blowing onto the

backed jib will then force the bow onto the new tack. As soon as the boat has gathered way on the new tack, the jib should be sheeted in normally to leeward.

Jibing. When running before the wind, the windward side of the boat can be changed by passing the stern through the eye of the wind as the mainsail moves over to the opposite side. This is jibing or wearing ship (Fig. 36). Jibing in a

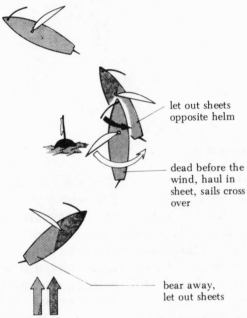

let out sheets
opposite helm

dead before the wind, haul in sheet, sails cross over

bear away, let out sheets

Fig. 36: Jibing

strong wind can be dangerous if badly done, causing many a centerboard boat to capsize and many a larger boat to be dismasted. If the boat has running backstays, they *must* be manned properly when jibing.

At the words "stand by to jibe" or "prepare to jibe," the main sheet hand checks that the sheet is ready to be hauled in quickly. "In main sheet," and he hauls it in rapidly and steadily until the boom is amidships, setting the leeward running backstay up tight as soon as he can. Meanwhile, the helmsman has borne away by putting the helm up until the boat is dead before the wind. The helmsman says, "jibe ho," and bears away a little more until the wind blows on the opposite side of the sail, which will fly over with a bang. Now the main sheet is paid out as fast as possible, as far as necessary for the new course, and the new leeward running backstay released, while the helmsman uses opposite helm to prevent the boat from luffing up violently.

In a centerboard dinghy, which has no backstays to be fouled by the boom as it lifts when jibing, it is usual and better to jibe all standing—that is to say, without pulling in the main sheet. If the main is pulled in hard, the dinghy tends to rush up into the wind after jibing and capsize because the main sheet cannot be let out again fast enough.

Man overboard. Occasionally a member of the crew falls overboard when the boat is underway, and you must know how to fish him out of the drink again. Man-overboard maneuvers (Figs. 37 and 38) are best practiced by throwing a floating object overboard. The moment the cry of "man overboard" is heard, it is essential to throw the horseshoe buoy or a life preserver *to* the victim but not *at* him. A closehauled boat (Fig. 37) then bears away, jibes, comes closehauled again, and shoots up into the wind, steering for the man (or the practice buoy) and picking him up. A boat that is sailing with the wind free (Fig. 38) luffs up, comes about, shoots up into the wind, and heads for the man. During all these maneuvers, one member of the crew must be detailed to keep an eye permanently on the man in the water while the boat is tacking or jibing, because a small head can very easily be lost in anything of a sea. Brightly colored clothing is a big aid to visibility and is much more easily spotted than dark clothes. It is very important to judge correctly the turning circle of the boat so that you reach the man with little or no way on. Having reached the man it is often very difficult to get him aboard again,

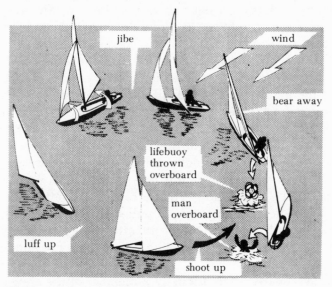

Fig. 37: Man overboard when closehauled

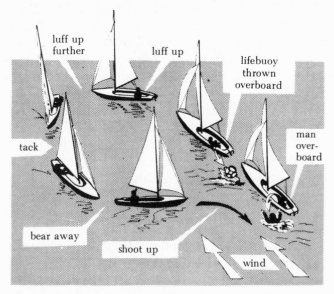

Fig. 38: Man overboard when running

especially if he is tired or unable to help himself. In dinghies it is easiest to clamber aboard over the stern. In larger boats with high topsides it is a help to lash a rope to the side so that he can put his foot in the bight and use his legs to help himself. It may even be necessary to use a tackle to get a heavy man on board again. If the boat has a swimming ladder, he can use that.

It is obviously wise to wear personal buoyancy; you should purchase it with care, and it should be of a type that will automatically float an unconscious person face upward. Children should always wear lifejackets and should be encouraged to learn to swim really well. The American Red Cross lifesaving and water safety courses are a great help and teach a child not to panic but to survive. Better still is not to fall overboard at all; deck shoes with special rubber soles that grip the deck are essential—ordinary rubber soles slip only too easily on shiny varnish or wet surfaces. In rough weather or when sailing alone, you should wear a safety harness that attaches you to the boat.

Carrying way. A large, heavy car is not set in motion as easily as a light one, but once the heavier car has started, it is, more difficult to slow and stop. Equally, it is more difficult to stop a large, heavy yacht with a deep keel than a light centerboard boat. In nautical language, a heavy boat carries more way. The most convenient method of reducing way is to sail directly into the wind; the wind then exerts no pressure on the sails, and the driving force is no longer in action; the engine, so to speak, is switched off. In addition, both headwind and water resistance brake the speed of the vessel. So, wherever possible, steer straight into the wind when picking up a buoy or making for a pier. Boats that carry a lot of way shoot a long distance before they lose all way and are stopped; they need far more room to stop than does a light centerboard boat, which carries little way and stops rapidly. When the wind is light, it has less braking effect, and a boat will shoot farther than when the wind is

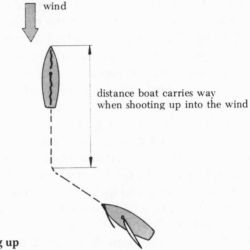

Fig. 39: Shooting up

stronger. You will need a good deal of experience before you can estimate accurately how far your boat will travel into the wind before stopping, for this distance varies tremendously under different weather conditions. Wind, tide, and sea all change from moment to moment so that you never have the same conditions to cope with twice—and this is half the fun of sailing.

Mooring. If you intend to pick up a buoy floating in the middle of a tideless stretch of water with a lot of room to maneuver, you can let the boat shoot straight up into the wind just as for the man-overboard maneuver (Fig. 37). If you are mooring alongside a pier or bridge, it is best to approach from leeward if possible. On the windward side the boats get bumped against the structure by wind and waves and can easily be damaged. Before coming alongside, the mooring lines should be prepared and the fenders (cushions made of rope, plastic, or cork, Fig. 43) put out over the side of the boat that is expected to come into contact with another boat or the pier. Bow and stern lines should be made fast to the pier or piles, breast lines

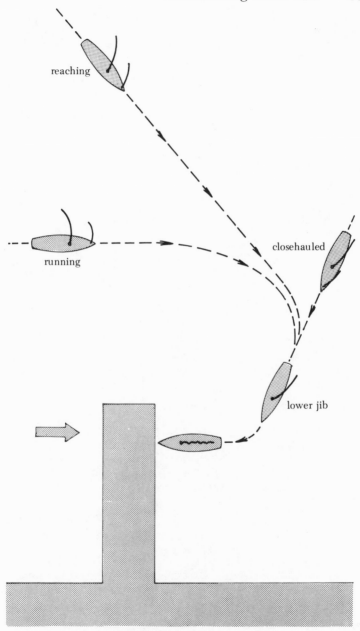

Fig. 40: Coming alongside with the wind at right angles to the pier

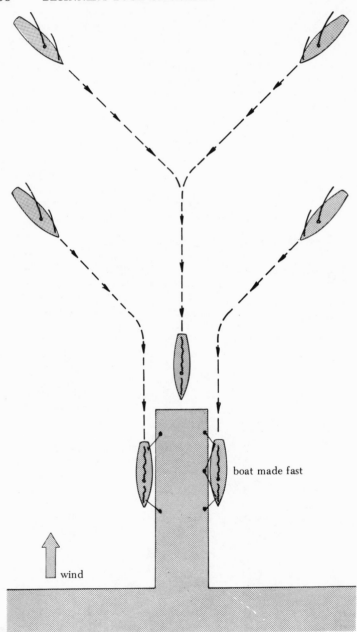

boat made fast

wind

Fig. 41: Coming alongside with the wind parallel to the pier

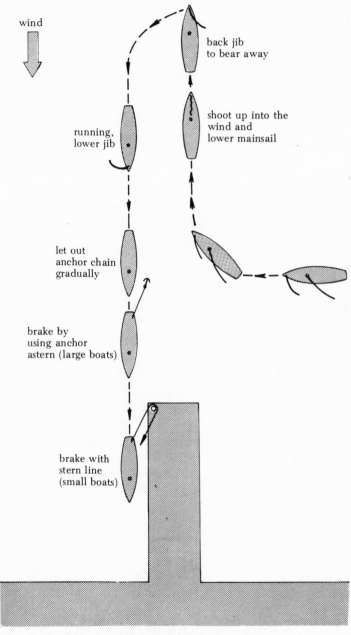

Fig. 42: Coming alongside under bare poles, braking

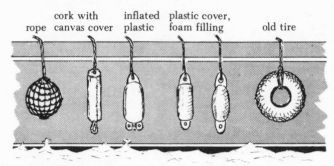

Fig. 43: Types of fenders

should be used to secure to a boat alongside, and spring lines should be used to keep two boats parallel.

When picking up a mooring buoy, your aim is to be stopped when you reach it. Therefore, in tidal waters or in a current, the effect of moving water must be taken into account. You may reach the buoy with no way on the boat, stopped in the water, but if the water itself is streaming past the buoy at a smart rate, your foredeck hand will part company either with the buoy he is trying to pick up or with the boat. Often other boats are moored nearby, and you can see from them how your boat will lie when her sails are off and the buoy safely aboard. If the boats are lying with their bows pointing toward the wind (wind-rode) or at any rate if the wind is forward of the beam, you should pick up your mooring under mainsail. On the other hand, if the tide is stronger than the wind, and the boats are lying with the wind abeam or anywhere aft of the beam, they are tide-rode, and you will be unable to let the mainsail out far enough to spill all the wind from it to come to a dead stop. In this case it is necessary to lower the mainsail well in advance, and then sail slowly up to the mooring against the tide under headsail only.

Warping.   It is often impossible to sail a boat directly into a chosen berth or slip. The best method then is either to anchor or to make fast to a convenient part of the pier, lower the sails, and then pull her to the berth by her mooring lines or warps. It may sometimes be necessary to run out an anchor to keep her stern away from the pier. In that case, the longest line aboard should be made fast to the stern of the boat and the anchor stowed in the dinghy with the rest of the line coiled neatly beside it. Someone should row the dinghy away from the yacht with short, quick strokes while the warp is payed out slowly, and the anchor should be thrown overboard attached to the end of the line when it has all been payed out. Large vessels usually anchor first to stow all sails and then move to the pier because their draft makes it difficult to maneuver in shallow water. And many large boats, of course, have auxiliary power for use in close quarters.

Anchoring. Here again, the boat must be brought almost to a standstill, either by shooting up into the wind if she is expected to be wind-rode at anchor, or by lowering the main and approaching against the tide under jib if she is expected to be tide-rode. In order to prevent fouling the flukes, the anchor should be thrown overboard when the boat is either moving very slowly ahead, or when she has just started to make sternway. The scope (the amount of chain or line let out) should be at least three times the depth of water at high tide, and the more chain that is run out, the better the anchor will hold.

There are two main types of anchor used by yachts: the yachtsman's or fisherman's and various patent anchors (Fig. 44). The stockless anchor is rarely used by small vessels. Before using the fisherman's anchor, the stock must be secured in the shank. Newer and more effective types of anchor are the danforth and the CQR or plow. All anchors must be shackled to the anchor chain and the shackle pin secured; alternatively, an anchor line can be attached with a fisherman's bend (Fig. 57) or with a round turn and two half hitches and the end seized (Fig. 52).

A boat lying at anchor heads either into the wind or

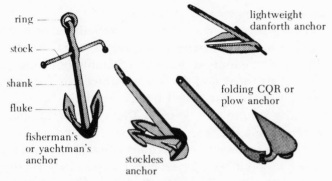

Fig. 44: Anchors

into the tide or current, and she swings to her anchor. If the wind changes or the tide turns, the boat swings in a different direction, and the chain dragging along the ground can foul the fluke of a fisherman's anchor, pulling it out of the bottom so that it no longer holds and the boat drifts. For safety, a crew member should keep an anchor watch, and if the wind increases or a heavy sea springs up a second anchor can be run out. A ship at anchor must display an anchor light at night.

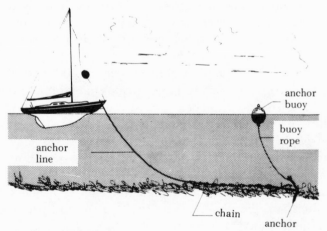

Fig. 45: A yacht at anchor

Casting off. How one casts off from a bridge, buoy, or pier depends on the circumstances and the direction of wind and tide. If the boat is lying to leeward of a pier, the sails can be hoisted and the bow pushed off so that the boat sails toward the open water. The helmsman puts the helm up, and the jib hand backs the jib if necessary. If the boat is on the windward side of the pier, it is best to maneuver her to the lee side by her mooring lines or else to run out an anchor and heave up on the chain until it is almost vertical and the boat lies in open water. Hoist sail quickly, pull up the anchor, and sail off. When leaving a buoy, if the wind is forward of the beam, all sails can be hoisted and the boat sailed off in the desired direction by backing the jib (Fig. 46). If the boat is tide-rode and the wind is aft of the beam,

hoist sails   back the   haul in sheets
                   jib   and set on course

Fig. 46: Leaving a buoy

it will not be possible to hoist the mainsail, so the boat is sailed away under headsail only; in open water, the boat is luffed into the wind and the mainsail hoisted.

It is a good idea for the skipper to discuss his plans with the crew beforehand so that they know what they have to do. The crew should obey the skipper's orders properly and quickly, even if the reason for them is unclear—most skippers have a very rough edge to their tongue, especially when performing a tricky maneuver under the eyes of yacht club critics!

Raising anchor. In order to raise the anchor (Fig. 47) when there is enough room to sail away freely, the boat is pulled up until the anchor chain is vertical. When ready to go, one last hard pull on the chain will veer the bow onto the chosen tack and break out the anchor, which is then hoisted and cleaned before being lashed on deck or stowed.

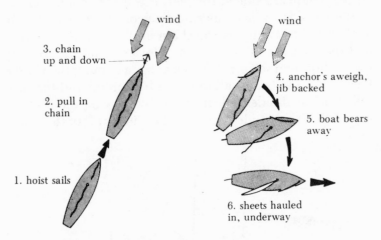

Fig. 47: Raising the anchor

Hoisting and lowering sail. When making ready aboard a large yacht, the sail cover must first be taken off the boom, rolled up, and stowed in its proper place below decks. The sail ties or sail stops, which are used to bundle up the sail and lash it to the boom, are taken off and the battens slipped into the batten pockets unless they are left in the pockets all the time. The main halyard is shackled to the head of the sail after the halyard man makes sure that it is clear and not tangled up with other halyards aloft. The main sheet is allowed to run free and the running backstays released so that the mainsail can slat back and forth when it has been hoisted. The headsail is attached at the tack to a fitting at the bow, the luff is hanked onto the forestay, the halyard is shackled to the head, and the headsail sheets are led through the blocks and shackled to the clew. If the boat is lying head-to-wind, the mainsail should be hoisted first, followed by the headsails.

Before lowering sails, it is important to check that the coils of the halyards have been capsized (turned over) so that the line can run freely without fouling or disappearing up the mast as the sail comes down. Sails should never be allowed to fall into the water when they are lowered. When lowering a gaff sail, the peak (Fig. 48), which is the highest point of the sail, should be lowered more slowly than the throat, which is attached to the lower part of the gaff at the mast. The mainsail should be lashed securely to the boom with ties and the cover put on so that an unexpected gale does not cause it to break loose.

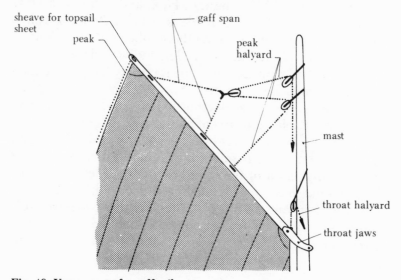

Fig. 48: Upper part of a gaff sail

Orders. All orders given on board should be clear and concise so that they are easily understood even when the wind is strong and it is hard to hear. Equally, any information from the foredeck such as "anchor up and down" or the depth of water when sounding should be clearly given and acknowledged.

7
Getting to Know Ropes and Knots

Tidiness and order aboard are extremely important. Space in a boat is inevitably very limited, so the golden rule is "a place for everything and everything in its place"—then it is ready to use when needed. Ropes and lines particularly must be carefully stowed, because only too easily can they get into a fearful bird's nest, or kink, and a line with kinks in it does not run through blocks easily. Rope, which is made of hemp, cotton, or synthetic fibers, is either laid by the maker or plaited like hair. The individual parts of laid rope are called strands; wire rope is usually laid left-handed and fiber rope right-handed. Now a number of synthetic fibers are used, such as dacron, nylon, terylene, and polypropylene. Each has different characteristics, and a suitable material can be found for every need on board. Tidying up lines is called coiling: small lines can be coiled by making rings or bights all of the same size over the left hand, but bigger lines have to be coiled on deck with the bights carefully laid one on top of the other. Right-handed rope must be coiled clockwise, and left-handed rope counterclockwise. In this country, nearly all line made specifically for sailboats is laid right-handed.

Hoisting. Light sails can be hoisted hand over hand by reaching up fairly high on the halyard, pulling down with one hand, and reaching up with the other. When the pull gets heavy, the halyard is passed around a cleat or belaying pin with a round turn and held firmly with one hand. The other hand grabs the taut vertical part of the halyard and all the weight of the body is thrown back, causing the sail to rise a bit higher. The extra bit of halyard is then pulled over the cleat and the process repeated until the sail is fully hoisted. Sweating up, as this is called, will sometimes need more than one person. On a boat of any size, a halyard should always be led around a winch during hoisting. Then, should the sail fill with wind prematurely, some very painful rope burns will be avoided.

Easing out. Before a line is eased out, the coil must be checked to see that it will run out freely. Easing must be done slowly, hand over hand, or by letting the line go around a winch or cleat, keeping some tension on it so that it can be checked at any moment. If you let a line out through your hands quickly without having taken a turn around something, you will burn your palms. No one should stand close to a coiled line or on it, for he could be knocked off his feet or overboard.

Knots. A sailor needs to know a number of knots to make things fast, to join lines together, or to make loops. Knots hold because the ropes grip each other tightly, and it is important to ensure that they do get a good grip when you learn to make them. The rule is that the left hand stays still while the right hand does the work. When natural fiber rope gets wet, it shrinks and becomes stiff and hard; as it dries, it stretches. Sailors' knots must hold whether wet or dry; they must neither come undone of their own accord nor jam so that they cannot be undone.

Granny knots. The granny, with which many a shoelace is tied, is *not* used on board. It is dangerous because it either jams or comes undone.

Figure-eight. A figure-eight knot (Fig. 49) is made at the end of a line to prevent it from running out of an eye or a block.

Fig. 49: Figure-eight knot

Fig. 50: Reef knot

Reef knot.   Reef knots (Fig. 50) are used to join together two lines of the same diameter. Both ends go out the same way as they came in so that they run parallel and the knot lies flat.

Fig. 51: Half hitch and two half hitches

Half hitch.   Half hitches (Fig. 51) are used only for short periods, and two half hitches should always be used. An anchor line can be fastened to the anchor ring by a round turn and two half hitches (Fig. 52), but the fisherman's bend (Fig. 57) is better for this purpose.

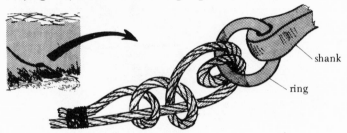

Fig. 52: **Round turn and two half hitches**

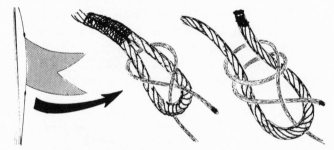

Fig. 53: **Sheet bend and double sheet bend**

Sheet bend.   The sheet bend and double sheet bend (Fig. 53) are used to join together two lines of unequal size. A line can also be attached to a rope eye in this way.

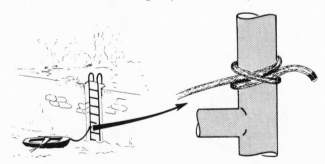

Fig. 54: **Clove hitch**

Clove hitch.   A clove hitch (Fig. 54) can be used to make a line fast to a bollard or to the rung of a ladder.

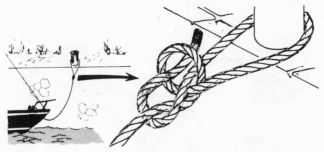

Fig. 55: Bowline

Bowline. The bowline is the most universally used sailor's knot. It is used to make a bight or loop in the end of a line where the bight is to remain a constant size (Fig. 55). It is therefore used for such jobs as making a bight on a mooring line. A double bowline (Fig. 56) is made with a doubled line.

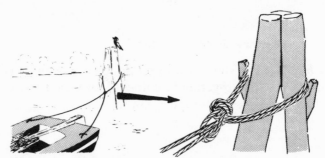

Fig. 56: Bowline on the bight

Fig. 57: Fisherman's bend

Fig. 58: Slippery hitch

Slippery hitch.   A slippery hitch (Fig. 58) can be used on a taut line, such as a sheet, if the hitch may need to be undone quickly.

Fig. 59: Whipping—Eye splice

Whipping.   Rope ends would fray quickly unless bound or finished in some way. Conventional rope is whipped (Fig. 59), but the ends of some light synthetic ropes can be welded by melting the fibers at the end with a match.

Splicing.   If two ropes are to be joined together permanently, they can be spliced together by weaving the individual strands into each other. A short splice thickens the rope and can be used only if the rope will not have to pass through a block or sheave. Alternatively, one can use a long splice, which does not increase the diameter of the rope. An eye splice is used to form an eye in a rope.

8
The Rules of the Road

International Regulations for the Prevention of Collisions at Sea. So that all vessels on the high seas can travel in safety, rules and regulations have been established internationally. These include steering and sailing rules for two vessels approaching each other, lights to be shown at night, signals in confined waters, sound signals in fog, distress signals, and so on. The regulations are not all compulsory for small pleasure yachts, and many do not apply on inland waters, but yachtsmen are subject to them and should carry a copy of the rules aboard.

Fortunately the basic right-of-way rules are the same in all waters—shipping lanes, the high seas, and most inland waters. When sailing in new waters it is always a good idea to check on the rules of the road in force, as well as on channels, currents, depth of water, and weather conditions.

Some rules have not changed: the boat that has right of way must not alter course and, if power-driven, must not alter speed until the danger of collision is past (Rule 21). A sailing or power-driven vessel that is overtaking another must always give way (Rule 24). The definition of an overtaking boat is one that approaches from any angle more than two points (22½°) abaft the other vessel's beam. In general, a power-driven vessel must keep clear of a vessel under sail (Rule 20). Here, however, there are obvious exceptions, for it is unreasonable to expect a large liner or tanker to alter course to avoid a small sailing dinghy or cruising boat. In many confined waters commercial traffic has right of way, and where large vessels are maneuvering in narrow, buoyed channels, small sailing boats should, as far as possible, keep clear of the dredged channels or at least keep to the sides of them. It is important not to sail heedlessly, hoping for the best—a collision in which you are to blame is very unpleasant.

Rules for sailboats.   Rule 17: When two sailing vessels are approaching one another so as to involve risk of collision, one of them shall keep out of the way of the other as follows:

(i) when each has the wind on a different side, the vessel that has the wind on the port side shall keep out of the way of the other (Fig. 60);

Fig. 60: Starboard tack has right of way.

(ii) when both have the wind on the same side, the vessel that is to windward shall keep out of the way of the vessel that is to leeward. For the purposes of this rule, the windward side shall be deemed to be the side opposite to that on which the mainsail is carried (Fig. 61).

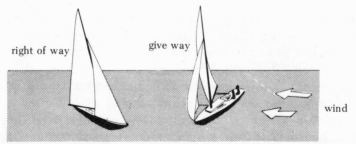

Fig. 61: Leeward boat has right of way.

Auxiliary engine. Many sailboats have auxiliary engines. Inland, and in dinghies, they are usually outboards used in flat calms to get the crew home on time, or perhaps on a hot, sunny, windless day to go for a swim—one of the rare occasions on which a sailor appreciates the fact that water has other uses than for sailing or for mixing with his rum. It is very pleasant if the engine decides to start. Not all of them do at the first attempt, for mostly the engine is allowed to laze and therefore revenges itself by going on strike. This does not mean that an outboard should be used too much at the expense of sailing, which is much more pleasant and above all much quieter, but an engine should be looked after and run from time to time.

Larger cruisers that voyage along the coast or put to sea can also use outboard motors, which must naturally be more powerful, since there is a greater weight to impel, but more usually they have a gasoline or diesel engine installed. This too must be looked after, run, and maintained, but it has one great advantage over the outboard—it cannot go to the bottom. Not surprisingly, an engine objects strongly to being drowned, and in order to prevent such a mishap, you should attach the outboard engine firmly to the boat by a line so that if it is dropped or comes adrift it will not disappear forever in the depths.

In addition to being a source of power in calms, an engine is useful when mooring a larger boat. Harbors are often very narrow and congested, and if you do not know the area, it is far wiser and safer to moor skillfully under power than to arrive out of control under sail. More damage is caused and more topsides ruined when mooring than at any other time. Casting off under sail is not so tricky, but unfortunately it is becoming so rare these days as engines are used more and more that it causes surprise among the bystanders.

Often sailboat skippers use sail and engine together in order to make better progress in light airs. The rules cover this combination and state (Rule 14) that in such a case the vessel must be treated as a power-driven vessel and behave as such as far as the rules of the road are concerned. Another point: it is not always possible to tell whether or not a vessel under sail is using her engine. Such a boat, therefore, must display the same lights as a power-driven vessel when traveling at night.

Power-driven vessels.   Rule 18: Two power vessels meeting. When two power-driven vessels are meeting head-on, or nearly head-on, so as to involve risk of collision, each shall alter her course to starboard so that each may pass on the port side of the other. This rule applies only to cases where vessels are meeting head-on, or nearly head-on, in such a manner as to involve risk of collision and does not apply to two vessels that must, if both keep on their respective courses, pass clear of each other.

Rule 19: Two power vessels crossing. When two power-driven vessels are crossing, so as to involve risk of collision, the vessel that has the other on her starboard side shall keep out of the way of the other.

Sound signals when altering course.   Rule 28: Power-driven vessels in normal visibility:

One short blast lasting about 1 second means "I am altering my course to starboard."

Two short blasts means "I am altering my course to port."

Three short blasts means "My engines are going astern."

On occasion you will hear one long blast lasting 5 or 6 seconds, which means "Be careful" or "Get out of my way." This is not in the rules, but you may encounter it in practice.

Sound signals for fog.   These are made by whistle, foghorn, or bell. Rule 15:

Whistle.   One prolonged blast at least every two minutes identifies a power-driven vessel making way through the water.

Two prolonged blasts at least every two minutes with a one-second interval between them identify a power-driven vessel underway, but stopped and making no way through the water.

One prolonged and two short blasts identify a vessel towing, a fishing vessel, or a vessel that is unable to maneuver to get out of the way. This is sounded every minute.

One prolonged and three short blasts identify the last of a line of boats being towed and is made every minute.

Foghorn.   One blast on the foghorn at least every minute identifies a sailing vessel underway on starboard tack.

Two blasts on the foghorn at least every minute identify a sailing vessel underway on port tack.

Three blasts in succession identify a sailing vessel with the wind abaft the beam.

Bell. A bell rung rapidly for five seconds at least every minute identifies a ship at anchor.

Three separate and distinct strokes before and after the five seconds' ringing of the bell mean the ship is aground.

The rules quoted are those you should know thoroughly because you will have to apply them frequently. There are many more signals and rules, and a copy of the full set of rules should be carried aboard so that you can refer to them when necessary.

9
Lights Carried by Ships

Lights must be carried by small sailboats when used at night. At least three are needed: one green, one red, and one white light ready to show. These lights should be exhibited by small boats for their own safety. Rule 1 states: All lights must be carried from sunset to sunrise.

Navigation lights. Navigation lights are carried by all vessels underway and consist of port, starboard, and stern lights, with the addition of masthead lights for power-driven vessels. On most inland lakes, no stern light is required, but it is always a good idea to have one. These must be visible at certain minimum distances laid down in the rules and are so constructed that they shine only over restricted sectors. They show the position of the ship and the direction in which she is moving.

Riding and special lights. Anchored vessels show a white riding light, while certain special vessels such as fishing boats with their nets out, ships unable to maneuver, cable-laying vessels, and pilot vessels carry special lights at night and shapes hung in the rigging by day so that they can be recognized at a distance. While navigation lights shine only over definite sectors, riding lights and those that differentiate between various types of vessels shine out all around the horizon.

Sidelights. Rule 2 (iv) and (v). Sidelights show from dead ahead to two points abaft the beam, an arc of 10 points or 112½°. The green light is carried to starboard, and the port light is red. Remember: port wine is red!

Mast lights. Rule 2(i): Mast lights are white and are carried on the mast by power-driven vessels and sailboats under power. They shine in an unbroken arc of 225° —that is, over the same arc as both sidelights—from two points abaft the beam to port, through dead ahead, to two points abaft the beam to starboard. These lights are generally mounted on sailboats two-thirds to' three-quarters of the way up the mast and should not be confused with the masthead light atop the mast, which shines out in all directions. The masthead light may be displayed at any time when underway and is generally used as an anchor light.

Stern light. Rule 10: The stern light covers the remaining arc of the horizon, namely from two points abaft the beam to port, through dead astern, to two points abaft the beam to starboard.

Sailing vessels. A sailing vessel underway carries green and red sidelights and a white stern light (Rules 5 and 10). As mentioned, this is optional on most inland lakes.

Power-driven vessels. A power-driven vessel underway carries sidelights and stern light (Rules 2(v) and (vi) and 10). In addition, she must carry a white light on her foremast, but if she is over 45.75 meters (150 feet) long, she must also carry a second light on her aftermast not less than 4.5 meters (15 feet) higher than the first (Rule 2(i), (ii), and (iii)).

Anchored vessels. A vessel at anchor carries a white riding light at night (Rule 11). A vessel over 45.75 meters long carries two riding lights at anchor, one forward and one aft (Rule 11).

Power-driven vessel towing. A power-driven vessel when towing carries, by day, a diamond shape in her rigging. At night, in addition to sidelights, she carries two white lights in a vertical line one over the other if she and the tow together measure less than 183 meters (600 feet), or three white lights one over the other if the total length is over 183 meters. She may also show a white light aft to make steering easier for the vessels towed. All vessels being towed show sidelights, and the last vessel shows a stern light in addition (Rule 3).

Vessels not under command. A vessel that is unmaneuverable and cannot therefore get out of the way carries two red lights in a vertical line one over the other, visible all around the horizon. By day, she carries two black balls (Rule 4). A vessel aground carries riding lights (Rule 11 (*a*) or (*b*)) and additionally two red lights vertically over each other. By day she carries three black balls (Rule 11 (*e*)).

Fishing boats.　Vessels trawling carry two lights vertically over each other, the upper one green and the lower white, both visible all around the horizon. Boats fishing, but not trawling, carry a red light above and a white light below. If fishing ·or trawling boats are making way through the water, they also show green and red sidelights and stern lights. If the outlying gear extends more than 153 meters (500 feet), they also carry an all-around white light placed in the direction of the outlying gear. By day small vessels hoist a fishing basket in the rigging, and larger vessels two cones with the points toward each other making an hourglass shape. If the gear extends more than 153 meters in the water, a black cone with the point upward is displayed in the direction of the outlying gear (Rule 9).

Other vessels.　A host of other lights and combinations of lights enable such vessels as wrecks, dredgers, and pilot vessels to be easily distinguished.

Action to avoid other vessels at night should always be

taken in good time, because the weak lights of small boats
are often seen very late; they are low on the water and can
be hidden by waves. When first coming on watch it is
important to check thoroughly on all the lights visible and
to consider what action may be necessary to avoid other
boats. If your own green starboard light is facing toward
the green sidelight of another vessel, or if your port light is
toward the port light of another ship, all is well.

When you see three lights ahead
Starboard wheel and show your red.

Green to green or red to red,
Perfect safety, go ahead.

If to starboard red appear
'Tis your duty to keep clear.
Act as judgment says is proper,
Port, or starboard, back, or stop her.

But when upon your port is seen
A steamer's starboard light of green,
There's not so much for you to do
For green to port keeps clear of you.

10
A Little Navigation

In order to sail a small boat safely up and down the coast or around in the Great Lakes, a knowledge of navigation and piloting is essential. The basic aids to navigation are a compass, charts, a ship's log, and a depth sounder or lead line.

The compass. The dry-card compass used on land is useless on board a tossing boat, because the needle swings about too wildly. A fluid compass, hung in gimbals, (Fig. 62) is used on yachts. Whereas the magnetic needle of a dry-card compass pivots freely on a point, a ship's compass has several magnets fastened under the compass rose so that the whole rose turns and points to magnetic north. The fluid in which such a compass floats is a mixture of alcohol and water, which damps the movement of the card and keeps it steady. The compass rose is divided into 32 points or 360° (see Fig. 1 and Appendix 3).

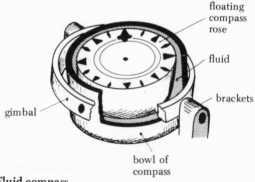

floating compass rose

fluid

brackets

gimbal

bowl of compass

Fig. 62: Fluid compass

Steering a compass course. Inside the bowl there are either one or two fixed vertical lines called lubber lines. The compass is installed in such a way that these lubber lines are parallel to the fore-and-aft line of the vessel. When steering a course, say 45°, northeast, the compass rose must be kept so that the lubber line (which represents the bow of the boat) is opposite 45°: the boat is then on course. A boat never keeps straight on course for long, and the compass rose turns continually to either side of the lubber line. If the rose turns so that the lubber line is to port of the correct course, say opposite 40°, then the bow has turned too far to port and the tiller should be put to port to bring her back on course.

Variation. The north point of a compass does not in fact point to true north (the North Pole): it points to magnetic north, a few degrees either to the east or west of true north. This difference is called variation and changes from place to place and from year to year. If the compass rose is pulled to the east of true north, variation is said to be easterly. The imaginary line of zero magnetic variation passes directly through the United States on a line running roughly from Chicago to Miami. Sailors in Lake Michigan or off the coast of Florida can all but forget variation. Sailors in New England must allow for westerly variation, while West Coast skippers must allow for easterly.

A compass rose appears on all navigational charts, and inside the true rose is a magnetic rose that points to magnetic north, allowing for variation at the date the chart was printed. A note along the east-west axis gives full details of variation at that place. Because variation differs from place to place, use the rose nearest the area in which you are working on the chart.

Deviation. Just as the compass is drawn away from true north to magnetic north, so it is influenced from on board by iron and steel fittings that draw it away from magnetic north. (You know already how you can pull a compass needle to one side with a piece of iron.) The deflection of the compass caused by metal on board is called deviation: it varies from boat to boat and also according to where the bow is pointing. Deviation, like variation, is said to be westerly or easterly and must be known for every course you steer. When the boat is put into commission, the compass must be swung and a deviation table drawn up. The table lists the deviation on every course. For example, if your course is 45° and the deviation table lists 3°W, it means that when you are steering 45° the compass is deflected 3° to the west of magnetic north by the metal on board. Once a deviation table has been drawn up, it is obviously important to see that no iron or steel is placed near the compass. A knife or a saucepan behind the bulkhead, for example, can alter the deviation.

To summarize: variation differs from place to place, but it is the same for every course steered from one particular place and for every boat at that place. Deviation is the same wherever the boat is, but it varies according to the course steered. It is different in every boat.

True course. When you draw a line on a chart representing the direction you intend to sail, you are drawing a true course, because a chart is drawn in relation to true north, and the lines of longitude on a Mercator chart run true north and south. But from the preceding paragraphs you will have realized that you *never* steer a true course.

Magnetic course. The magnetic course is found by applying variation to the true course, either by adding westerly variation or by subtracting easterly variation. For example, if your true course is 250° and your variation is 5°W, the magnetic course is 255°.

Compass course. The compass course is the course to

steer, and it is determined by applying both variation and deviation to the true course. Just as is the case with variation, westerly deviation is applied by adding, and easterly by subtracting. If your true course is 250°, your variation is 5°W (add), and your deviation is 3°E (subtract), the compass course is 252°.

Tides and tidal streams.   A tide is the rise and fall of the level of the sea—a vertical movement of water. There are two tides a day, and the difference in height between high tide and low tide is called the range. At neap tides the range is small; at spring tides the range is great, and more land is covered at high water and more of the seabed is uncovered at low water.

A tidal stream is a horizontal movement of water caused by the vertical movement of the tide. At neaps the tidal streams run less strongly than at spring tides. The rising tide is the flood, and the falling tide is the ebb.

When you plot a course, you must allow for the effect of a tidal stream or current; details of these can be found in tide tables, charts, and nautical almanacs.

Leeway.   You must allow for leeway, too, for a boat does not always sail exactly along the line of the course steered. If she is running dead before the wind, she will make no leeway because all the thrust of the wind is pushing her along her course. But as the wind comes farther and farther ahead, it will push her increasingly sideways as well as forward, and she will sail through the water at an angle to the course being steered. This angle is the leeway and can be estimated by looking at the wake of the log line, which will not stream out exactly astern, but at an angle.

Plotting a course (Fig. 63).   Suppose that you want to sail from A to B along the line drawn on the chart, which is 250° true. You measure the length of AB in the side margin with dividers and find that it is four nautical miles. Your

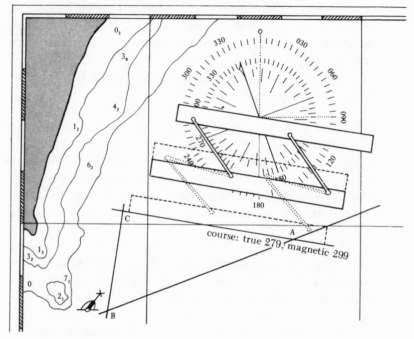

Fig. 63: Plotting a course

boat is sailing at four knots so she will take one hour to
cover the distance. Looking up the tidal stream details, you
find that for the next hour its direction is 190° and that it
will be running at 2 knots, so you draw a line from point B
in exactly the opposite direction to that of the tidal stream,
namely at 10°. You cut this line off at two miles at point C,
because the tidal stream is expected to run at two knots.
The true course you will need to steer to make good AB on
the chart is AC. You can allow for leeway in the same way.
You intend to sail along the line AC, the true course: this
must now be adjusted for variation and deviation to find
the course to steer. Unless the chart is very old, you can
forget about variation if you use the central or magnetic
rose on the chart, which is already adjusted for variation.
Using parallel rules, carry the line AC over to the nearest

rose by first holding one half of the ruler steady on the chart while you open the other out, then holding the second half steady while you close the first up to it. Opening out again, you can reach the center of the roses and read off the degrees of the magnetic course on the magnetic rose: 299°. Now apply deviation. Looking up the table, you find that deviation on a course of NW + W is 3°W. Westerly deviation must be added, so the course to steer—the compass course—will be 302°.

Converting bearings and courses. So far we have converted from true to magnetic to compass, but when converting compass bearings and courses to magnetic, or magnetic to true, easterly and westerly deviation and variation are applied in the opposite direction. So, when converting

From True to Magnetic to Compass: westerly deviation and variation must be added; easterly must be subtracted.

From Compass to Magnetic to True: westerly deviation and variation must be subtracted; easterly must be added.

Charts. Practically all charts are Mercator charts, which reproduce the curved surface of the earth on paper accurately as far as angles are concerned: a straight line drawn on a Mercator chart is in reality a curve on the earth's curved surface. To "flatten" the earth's surface, the lines of longitude on the chart get farther apart toward the poles. To keep the proportions right, the distance between the degrees of latitude also increases slightly on the chart toward the poles, and if you look at a map of the whole earth in an atlas using Mercator projections, you will see that Greenland and land near the poles appear to be vast continents because the lines of latitude and longitude are more widely spaced than near the equator.

Nautical miles.   A nautical mile is 1852 meters long (6080 feet or 1.15 statute or land miles) and is the length of one minute of the earth's circumference at the equator, latitude 0°. As the circumferences of the lines of latitude decrease toward the poles, the length of a minute of longitude also decreases. By contrast, the circumferences of the lines of longitude around the earth passing through both poles are all the same and the same as that of the equator. A minute of latitude is therefore always a nautical mile, as on the side margins of charts. As mentioned before, the distance on the chart between degrees of latitude does increase slightly toward the poles, and measurements should always be taken along the vertical margin of the chart in the same latitude as the area you are using on the chart.

Symbols.   As the sailor is concerned mainly with the sea, only those objects on land that are particularly conspicuous and that can be used for taking bearings or as points to steer for, are marked on a chart. Land on charts is colored yellow, and water is colored blue and white.

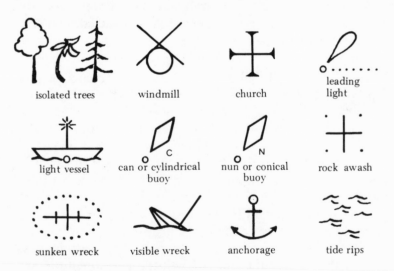

Fig. 64: Symbols used on charts

Charts also give information on a tremendous number of subjects such as tides, tidal streams, dangers, quality of the bottom (gravel, rock, sand, mud), buoyage, lights, and much else. Depths of water are shown by soundings in feet or fathoms at low water levels at chart datum.

Ship's position.   The ship's position is described by latitude and longitude, for example: 50° 29' N, 2° 27' W. Naturally it is not usually possible to tell the exact position of a vessel merely by looking at the chart. You can fix your position by using objects such as buoys or landmarks, the exact positions of which are shown on the chart. If no land is in sight, or if no convenient objects are visible, your position has to be estimated by dead reckoning (DR)—that is, by estimating the course made good and the distance run since the last known position, taking into account the course steered, leeway, and the effects of the tidal stream.

Bearings.   Fixing a ship's position using landmarks or buoys is done by taking bearings on them. A bearing is the direction of one object in relation to another, in this case the direction of an object in relation to the ship. Small boats can best take a bearing by steering straight for the object, when the course steered will also be the compass bearing of the object. The compass bearing is then corrected for deviation (add easterly, subtract westerly). To enter this magnetic bearing on the chart, use the nearest rose, lay the parallel rule across it from the center to the magnetic bearing, and then carry this over to the object on which the bearing was taken and pencil a line to seaward along it. The boat's position is somewhere along that line. In most larger boats a hand bearing compass (Fig. 65) or a ring sight is used. When the object, the sights, and the lubber line are all in line, the compass reading is noted. Deviation is applied only when the steering compass is used. When using a hand bearing compass, stand well away from the influence of any iron fixtures such as the engine.

Fig. 65: Hand bearing compass

Cross bearings. One bearing alone cannot fix the ship's position. It is only by taking cross bearings (Fig. 66)—that is, two bearings of well-separated objects—that you can

bearing A   bearing B

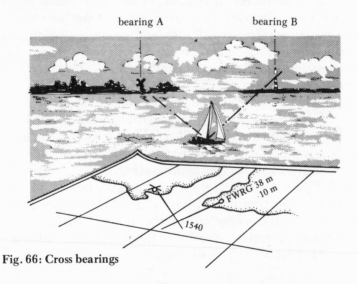

Fig. 66: Cross bearings

find the position. The boat is at the point where the bearings cross. The closer a boat is to the objects, the more accurate the fix will be. If the two bearings meet at an angle of less than 30° or more than 150°, the fix is unreliable. It is far better to take three bearings and know that the boat will be in the resulting triangle.

Running fix. When only one object is visible, the position can be found by taking a running fix (Fig. 67). First take a

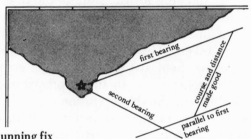

Fig. 67: Running fix

bearing and note the time; then steer a steady course. Take a second bearing when the angle of the object has changed greatly, note the time again, and enter both bearings on the chart. The course and distance made good are estimated by dead reckoning and are then entered on the chart from any point on the first bearing. Through the end of the line that represents course and distance made good, draw a line parallel to the first bearing. The ship's position is where this line cuts the second bearing.

Log. To take a running fix it is necessary to know the distance run. A taffrail log can be used to measure the distance a boat sails through the water by means of a propeller towed on a line behind the ship. This rotates, working the log register, and you can read the distance sailed on the dial of the register. Modern electronic equipment includes combined speed and distance indicators that give the speed of the boat at any moment as well as the distance sailed.

Lead. In poor visibility or fog, when you cannot take bearings, it is possible to get an idea of your position by sounding with the lead. The lead is just that: a lump of lead on the end of a line, hollowed out underneath so that it can be "armed" by putting a lump of tallow or grease in it to bring up a sample of the bottom. Charts give details of the bottom.

You can take a series of soundings at regular intervals while holding a steady course. The soundings are corrected to chart datum, allowing for the state of the tide; they are then drawn to the same scale as the chart on a piece of paper, along a line representing the distance run while soundings were taken. The piece of paper is then moved about on the chart, held at the angle of the course made good, until it matches up with the depths shown on the chart, thus establishing the ship's position.

The lead line is marked at intervals with different materials. When sounding, the lead must be thrown well forward to allow for the speed of the boat through the water and the depth noted when the line is straight up and down alongside the leadsman.

Many yachts now are equipped with an echo sounder that establishes the depth of water by sending an impulse that travels to the bottom and is echoed back to the receiver. The depths can be read directly off a dial.

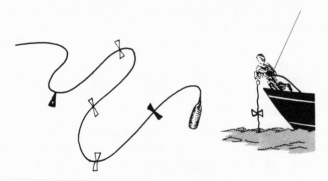

Fig. 68: Sounding

11
Buoys and Lights

Buoys, lighthouses, fog signals, and other aids to navigation are maintained by the federal government on coastal waters, rivers and other waters navigable from the sea, and bodies of water that do not lie entirely within the boundaries of one state. State or local governments or even companies or persons may maintain "private" aids to navigation. All such aids mark channels, harbor mouths, shoals, obstructions, and other features or dangers in the waters.

The number of aids to navigation in any area will depend on the amount of traffic. A main channel that is used night and day will be fully buoyed and lighted, for example, while a minor channel may be only partly buoyed and lighted.

Among the federal, state, and private aids to navigation, you will find a great and confusing variety of buoys, towers, lights, and other markers. To add to the confusion, the Intracoastal Waterway and the Western Rivers have systems that differ from the one you will learn here. When navigating in strange waters, it is important to use your chart, which will locate and describe each aid.

Buoys. Buoys and markers are of several kinds: cans, which are cylindrical in shape, and nuns, which are cylindrical with cone-shaped tops. In addition, some buoys look like small skeleton towers floating on the water. Buoys aid the navigator by their distinctive colors, shapes, lights, and sounds (bells and gongs).

The lateral system. Buoys and markers vary from country

to country. Basically there are two systems of buoy-age—cardinal and lateral—and the lateral system is used in the United States in all waters under federal jurisdiction. The basic principle of the lateral system can be summarized in the phrase "red right returning," meaning that when you enter a channel from seaward (returning from sea), you take red markers to your starboard (right) side. Black markers will be on your port side. The opposite is true when leaving a channel and going to sea—you take black markers to starboard and red to port.

Fig. 69: Channel buoys

It is easy to tell which side is "seaward" when you enter a harbor or bay. It is not so easy when you encounter a channel that runs along a coast, so certain conventions are adopted to designate the "seaward" direction: you are considered to be coming from seaward (or "returning") in a southerly direction along the Atlantic coast, in a northerly or westerly direction on the Gulf coast, and in a northerly direction on the Pacific coast. In the Great Lakes, from seaward is from the outlet end of each lake.

Starboard side of a channel. The starboard side of a

channel, when entering from seaward, may be marked with any of the following: a red nun, a red or white flashing or quick flashing light, or a triangular "daymark" shape. If the nun is numbered, it will have an even number, and numbers will increase as you proceed from seaward.

Port side of a channel.   The port side of a channel, when entering from seaward, may be marked by a black can, a green or white flashing or quick flashing light, or a square daymark shape. If the can is numbered, it will have an odd number, and numbers will increase from seaward.

Channel junction or obstruction.   A channel junction or an obstruction that you may pass on either side (with fairly wide berth) may be marked by a red-and-black horizontally striped nun or can; a green, red, or white interrupted quick flashing light; or a triangular or square daymark. The preferred side—the one on which to pass if possible—is indicated by the color of the top stripe of the buoy or the color of the light. (If the top stripe is black or the light is green, try to pass with the buoy to your port side.)

Middle of a channel.   Midchannel buoys, which mark the middle of a channel like a centerline on a road, are nuns or cans that have vertical black and white stripes and may also have white lights. You should pass fairly close by them on either side.

Wrecks and hazards.   In addition to marking channels, nuns and cans are used to mark rocks, shoals, wrecks, and other hazards in the waters. Follow the same rules for passing these buoys—when going from seaward, take red buoys to starboard.

Lights.   Lighthouses, lightships, light floats, buoys, and beacons all have individual characteristics so that there can be no confusion about which light you are seeing. All lights at sea flash or occult so that they will not look like the navigation lights of a ship. Fixed lights are only found on shore and on vessels. Full details of the characteristics of lights can be found on charts, in nautical almanacs, and in the light lists.

Lights are red (R), white (W), and green (G), as explained. They shine or flash in patterns called light phase characteristics.

Fixed lights (abbreviation on charts, F) shine uninterruptedly.

Occulting lights (Occ) shine steadily for some time, followed by an eclipse that is always shorter than the light.

Flashing lights (Fl) show one flash at regular intervals. The darkness always lasts longer than the light. Flashes occur less than 30 times per minute.

Quick flashing (Qk Fl) lights flash continuously very quickly.

Group flashing (Gp Fl) and **Group occulting** (Gp Occ) lights show groups of lights followed by eclipses.

Alternating flashing lights (Alt Fl) show flashes of alternating colors—white and red or white and green.

Equal interval lights (E Int) show equal periods of light and darkness.

Fixed and flashing lights (F and Fl) are fixed lights showing a brighter flash at regular intervals.

Sectors. Many lights show different colors in different sectors, the white sector normally being the safe one (Fig. 70), or have the light obscured or invisible in certain sectors. Your chart will detail such light characteristics.

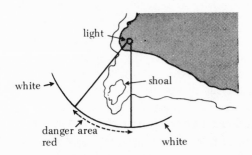

Fig. 70: Sectored light

12
Weather

Everyone is affected by the weather, particularly the sailor, who cannot move without wind, cannot see in fog, and needs warning of storms to come. Weather forecasts and maps appear on television, in some daily papers, and are now broadcast twenty-four hours a day by the United States government on a frequency of 162.55 MHz from a network of stations that can be heard through most of North America.

There are two main types of weather: stable, settled weather associated with anticyclones, and unsettled, changeable weather with conditions varying from day to day and hour to hour as depressions or lows pass by. The positions of anticyclones and lows can be seen on weather maps, which are maps with lines called isobars drawn on them. These isobars join all those places at which atmospheric pressure is the same, just as contour lines join all those places that are the same height above sea level. Widely spaced isobars show a gradual change in pressure; closely spaced isobars show a sudden change.

An anticyclone is like a plateau of high pressure, often extending over an enormous area and drifting slowly. The weather in the central part is fine and settled, with light winds for days on end; toward the edges of a high-pressure area, long-lasting strong winds may blow.

In contrast, depressions are like counterclockwise whirlpools with closely spaced isobars around a small center of low pressure. The wind blows more strongly nearer the center, and the lower the central pressure, the fiercer the gale will be. Lows move rapidly and often follow each other in quick succession. To the south of the center is a warm front, followed by a more rapidly moving cold front, which catches up the warm front, forming what is called an occluded front. Throughout most of North America, weather patterns tend to move from west to east—warm fronts in a northerly direction, cold fronts in a southerly one. Tropical storms in the South Atlantic states and Gulf areas are a big exception to this rule.

Warning of the approach of a depression and its attendant gales is given by cirrus (mares' tails) clouds, showing a strong wind high in the sky. The barometer, an instrument that registers atmospheric pressure, starts to fall, the sky clouds over, and it starts to rain while the wind increases in strength until a strong wind or gale is blowing, depending on the vigor of the low. Behind the center, the sky gradually clears and the wind slowly eases as the barometer rises. The way in which the wind direction alters as a depression passes can be seen in Fig. 71. If the center is to the north, the winds will veer from south to southwest (A), while if the center is to the south, the winds will back from southeast to northeast (B). The wind is said to veer

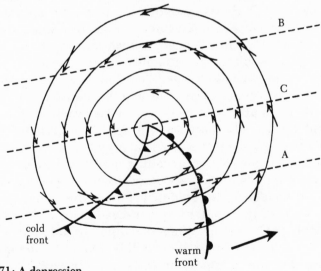

Fig. 71: A depression

when it changes in a clockwise direction, to back when it changes in a counterclockwise direction. If the center passes overhead, the wind direction remains constant as it approaches, but the strength increases greatly as the barometer falls. The center itself is calm, and after it has passed the wind blows as strongly as or more strongly than before from the opposite direction, while the barometer rises, promising better weather to come.

Weather forecasting is far from easy, even for the expert meteorologist, and the sailor must use his own observation and experience of local conditions. The barometer is particularly important and should be read regularly and checked and reset for accuracy according to local weather broadcasts. Slow rises promise fine weather, while sharp falls foretell strong winds. Different types of cloud are likely to be followed by different weather conditions: mares' tails precede a depression; a red sky at night and a gray dawn herald a fine day. Thunderclouds in particular should be watched, for they bring violent and often dangerous squalls in an otherwise peaceful day.

Observation is very important, and one advantage of racing is that the skipper quickly learns to note and interpret signs of wind, seas, and tide, and to make the best use of what he has noticed. Smoke blowing from distant chimneys or boats sailing a mile or two away may give warning of a wind change. The shallower the water, the shorter and steeper seas will be and the more easily they will break, so an area of breaking water may well mean a shoal. Breaking seas also occur in rip tides (choppy and violent narrow paths of water coursing at approximately 90 degrees to the direction of the prevailing waves and caused by an underwater obstruction, shoal, or beach) or where there are sudden changes in the contours of the seabed. Such changes are frequently found by major headlands such as Point Fermin or Cape Ann. When the wind and tide are moving in the same direction, the sea will be relatively smooth, but when they are in opposition the seas are noticeably bigger and more vicious. Keep an eye open in hazy weather for signs of the coast disappearing in the distance as sea fog approaches.

There are many jingles that were made up years ago to warn a skipper what to expect. The red sky in the morning is as much the sailor's warning as the shepherd's. Some of the most useful are:

> First rise after low
> Foretells a stronger blow.
> Long foretold, long last
> Short notice, soon past.
>
> Haloes round the moon or sun
> Rain before the day is done.
>
> If the rain comes before the wind
> Sails and halyards you must mind;
> When the wind's before the rain
> Hoist your topsail up again.
>
> At sea with low and falling glass
> Soundly sleeps the careless ass,
> Only when it's high and rising
> Truly rests the careful wise one.

13
Sea Legs

Every child is born into the world with a pair of legs, but sea legs that can be trusted can be acquired only by going to sea. The man with proper sea legs (the envy of all landlubbers) moves about surely and quickly on a steeply angled, heaving deck; he is immune to seasickness and rolls like a ship at sea on returning to land after a long voyage.

There are occasions when even old sea dogs are sick, but it does not worry them greatly; they keep up their spirits and accept the purely physical discomfort (which, after all, occurs at times on land as well as at sea) with humor and resignation. It is important to have no fear of being sick, for psychological factors play their part—it is even possible to make an inexperienced sailor ill in harbor by telling him horror stories about seasickness. The man who worries about sickness will surely be laid low by it.

Strong-minded people are very rarely sick, and if for once they do fall by the wayside, they grin and bear it and work on. How do you avoid being sick? Above all don't worry about it. Stay out in the fresh air and keep busy with some diverting occupation if sickness threatens, for being busy is the best prevention. It takes your mind off your queasiness. Eat well but sensibly—fatty food is disastrous—and do not turn up your nose at a spot of alcohol, though too much is fatal. Never look at the waves heaving up and down near the ship, but look far out over the horizon.

Remember, however, that many people do have honest problems with illness in a rough sea. It is a wise skipper who asks before taking people out and, if they have a history of a problem, recommends one of the many dramamine-type seasick aids available.

14
Racing

Many sailors enjoy competition. Boats of all sizes and classes race—dinghies, cruisers, and racing yachts alike. There are races such as the America's Cup and the One Ton Cup for which boats are specially built, but this is naturally very expensive, and most yachtsmen cannot afford to have a boat designed specifically for one race. Before entering a race, a boat should be thoroughly tuned so that the crew can get the best out of her on all points of sailing. And the crew should be thoroughly trained so that all sail handling will be done quickly and efficiently.

Ocean racing. There are two main types of races: one-design racing over a buoy-marked course, in which all boats are competing only against boats of identical size and/or design; and offshore handicap racing, in which larger cruiser/racers may compete with one another under a handicap formula that seeks to level differences in size and shape. Off shore handicap races may be either over buoy-marked courses or from one point to another. There are a number of famous long-distance races such as the 635-mile-long Bermuda race (now 672 miles long), which is run every two years and alternates with the 615-mile-long Fastnet race. The oldest and longest ocean race is the Transatlantic race, which was first sailed in 1866 and which is about 3,000 miles long.

Dinghy racing. The term *dinghy* is greatly misunderstood on this side of the Atlantic, where it is often applied to any small rowboat that is used to reach a larger sailboat. In fact, the term applies to any sailboat that is raced as a one-design and that carries no cruising or overnight ac-

101

commodations. In racing circles in the United States, the smaller one-designs are the boats commonly called dinghies. Dinghy races last two or three hours over a course about ten miles long. The course is usually triangular so that the boats have to beat, reach, and run. The three legs may total far less than ten miles, in which case the boats sail two or more times around the course. While in an ocean race there is only one race and the winner is the first boat on corrected time, in dinghy and small boat events there are often a number of races over the same or nearly the same course, either at different times or on different days. Each race has its individual winner and second and third placers, and these standings count toward the determination of the winner of the series as a whole.

There are virtually no professionals as in other sporting activities, and money prizes play little part. The aim is to win a National, North American, or World Championship, to win an Olympic medal, or just to win the local weekend race at the club.

Class racing.   Boats usually race against others of the same class; in one-design classes the boats are identical, and in restricted classes they are very similar to each other, so that the result of the race depends on tuning, sailing ability, and knowledge of the racing rules—not to mention occasional good luck.

Handicap racing.   Larger yachts that are not identical or built to any particular set of regulations race against each other in handicap races. There are several handicap systems, the aim of all of which is to even out the differences of age, speed, size, and design so that the boats can race against each other fairly, each with a chance of winning. The handicap is applied on the basis of the time taken to complete the course, or sometimes on the distance sailed. When the time taken to complete the course is known, it is adjusted under the handicap system to produce what is called the corrected time. The winner is the boat that has taken the least corrected time.

Racing rules.   Dinghy and round-the-buoys racing often produce large fleets in close quarters. The normal collision rules are not adequate for the cut-and-thrust of close racing, so a very detailed set of rules has been drawn up by the North American Yacht Racing Union (NAYRU) to ensure that boats do not collide with each other or hinder each other, except as allowed under the rules. The most important are the right-of-way rules, which lay down precisely how boats must act when overtaking, meeting, rounding marks, and so on. Basically they do not conflict with the normal rules of the road, except that a boat being overtaken to windward is allowed to defend by luffing the overtaker. This would be unthinkable and dangerous under normal circumstances, but it is allowed when racing. A thorough knowledge of the NAYRU rules gives opportunities to use them tactically to beat another boat and, together with the purely physical effort involved, is one of the main attractions of dinghy and small-boat racing. The racing rules do not play quite such an important part in ocean racing, where there are usually fewer competitors spread out over a vast expanse of water, very often not seeing each other between the start and the finish. Ocean races are won more by sailing ability, good navigation, and a thorough knowledge of the sea and weather conditions.

Appendix 1

Extracts from the International Regulations for the Prevention of Collisions at Sea

Power-driven vessel

Rule 2(a) i: On or in front of the foremast or in the forepart of the vessel a white light so constructed as to show an unbroken light over an arc of the horizon of 225° (20 points of the compass), so fixed as to show the light 112½° (10 points) on each side of the vessel, that is from right ahead to 22½° (2 points) abaft the beam on either side, and of such a character as to be visible at a distance of at least 5 miles.

Rule 2 (a) ii: Either forward or abaft the white light mentioned above a second white light similar in construction and character to that light. Vessels of less than 45.75 meters (150 feet) in length shall not be required to carry this second light but may do so.

Rule 2 (a) iv: On the starboard side a green light so constructed as to show an unbroken light over an arc of the horizon of 112½° (10 points), so fixed as to show the light from right ahead to 22½° (2 points) abaft the beam on the starboard side, and of such a character as to be visible at a distance of at least 2 miles.

Rule 2 (a) v: On the port side a red light similar to (iv) above but showing from right ahead to 22½° (2 points) abaft the beam on the port side.

Rule 10: Stern light. A vessel when underway shall carry at her stern a white light so constructed that it shall show an unbroken light over an arc of the horizon of 135° (12 points), so fixed as to show the light 67½° (6 points) from right aft on each side of the vessel, and of such a character as to be visible at a distance of at least 2 miles.

Sailing vessel

Rule 5 (a): A sailing vessel underway . . . shall carry the same lights as are prescribed in Rule 2 for a power-driven vessel with the exception of the white lights specified therein which she shall never carry. She shall also carry a stern light as specified in Rule 10. . .

Small sailing or rowing vessels of less than 12.20 meters (40 feet) in length

Rule 7 (d): If they do not carry sidelights, shall carry where it can best be seen a lantern showing a green light on one side and a red light on the other, of such a character as to be visible at a distance of at least one mile and so fixed that the green light shall not be seen on the port side, nor the red light on the starboard side. Where it is not possible to fix this light it shall be kept ready for immediate use. . . .

Small rowing boats

Rule 7 (f): Small rowing boats whether under oars or sail shall only be required to have ready at hand an electric torch or a lighted lantern showing a white light which shall be exhibited in sufficient time to prevent collision.

Power-driven vessels of less than 19.80 meters (65 feet) in length

Rule 7 (a) i: In the forepart of the vessel at a height above the gunwale of not less than 2.75 meters (9 feet) a white light constructed as prescribed in Rule 2 (a) i, and visible at least 3 miles.

Rule 7 (a) ii: Green and red sidelights as prescribed in Rule 2 (a) iv, visible at least one mile, or a combined lantern as prescribed in Rule 7 (d) not less than 0.91 meters (3 feet) below the white light.

Rule 10: A white stern light visible at least 2 miles.

Rule 7 (c): Power-driven vessels of less than 12.20 meters (40 feet) in length may carry the white light at a lesser height than 2.75 meters (9 feet) above the gunwale, but it shall be carried not less than 0.91 meters (3 feet) above the sidelights or the combined lantern prescribed in Rule 7 (a) ii.

Vessel under sail—using power also

Rule 14: A vessel proceeding under sail, when also being propelled by machinery, shall carry in the daytime forward, where it can best be seen, one black conical shape, point downward, not less than 2 feet in diameter at its base.

Rule 1 (c) iv: Every vessel under power, whether under sail or not, is to be considered a power-driven vessel. (At night therefore she must carry sidelights, stern light and masthead light.)

Vessels at anchor

Rule 11 (a): A vessel of less than 45.75 meters (150 feet) when at anchor shall carry in the forepart of the vessel where it can best be seen a white light visible all round the horizon at a distance of at least 2 miles.

Rule 11 (c): Between sunrise and sunset every vessel when at anchor shall carry in the forepart of the vessel one black ball not less than 2 feet in diameter.

Vessels not under command

Rule 4 (a): A vessel which is not under command shall carry in lieu of masthead lights two red lights in a vertical line one over the other not less than 1.83 meters (6 feet) apart visible all round the horizon at a distance of at least 2 miles. By day two black balls or shapes.

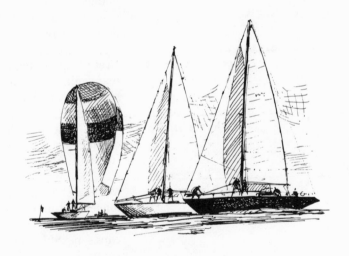

Appendix 2

The Beaufort Wind Scale

Beaufort Number	Description	Sea criterion
0	Calm	Sea like a mirror
1	Light air	Small wavelets like scales but no foamy crests
2	Light breeze	Wavelets more pronounced. Crests have glassy appearance but do not break
3	Gentle breeze	Crests begin to break, foam glassy, a few scattered whitecaps
4	Moderate breeze	Waves small but becoming longer, more frequent whitecaps
5	Fresh breeze	Moderate waves, longer and more pronounced, many whitecaps, possibly some spray
6	Strong breeze	Large waves start to form, white foam crests more extensive, some spray

Land criterion	Wind speed knots	meters per second
Smoke rises vertically	under 1	0.0—0.2
Direction of wind can be seen by smoke but not vanes	1—3	0.3—1.5
Wind felt on face, vanes move, leaves rustle	4—6	1.6—3.3
Leaves and small twigs in motion, small flags extended	7—10	3.4—5.4
Dust raised, loose paper blown about, small branches in motion	11—16	5.5—7.9
Small broad-leaved trees begin to sway, whitecaps on inland waters	17—21	8.0—10.7
Large branches in motion, telegraph wires whistle, umbrellas awkward to handle	22—27	10.8—13.8

Beaufort Number	Description	Sea criterion
7	Near gale	Longer and higher waves, foam blown in streaks from breaking crests
8	Gale	Moderately high waves, foam blown in dense streaks
9	Strong gale	High waves, dense streaks, crests begin to topple over
10	Storm	Very high waves with long overhanging crests, sea white with foam, visibility affected
11	Violent storm	Exceptionally high waves, visibility much affected
12	Hurricane	Air is filled with foam and spray, the sea is completely white, visibility very much affected

Land criterion	Wind speed knots	meters per second
Whole trees in motion	28—33	13.9—17.1
Twigs broken off trees, progress difficult	34—40	17.2—20.7
Slight damage to houses (loose shingles)	41—47	20.8—24.4
Considerable damage to buildings, trees up-rooted	48—55	24.5—28.4
Widespread damage	56—63	28.5—32.6
Widespread damage	over 64	32.7—36.9

Appendix 3

Points of the Compass

(clockwise)

North North by East **North-Northeast** Northeast by North **Northeast** Northeast by East **East-Northeast** East by North

East East by South **East-Southeast** Southeast by East **Southeast** Southeast by South **South-Southeast** South by East

South South by West **South-Southwest** Southwest by South **Southwest** Southwest by West **West-Southwest** West by South

West West by North **West-Northwest** Northwest by West **Northwest** Northwest by North **North-Northwest** North by West

Appendix 4

Parts of the Boat

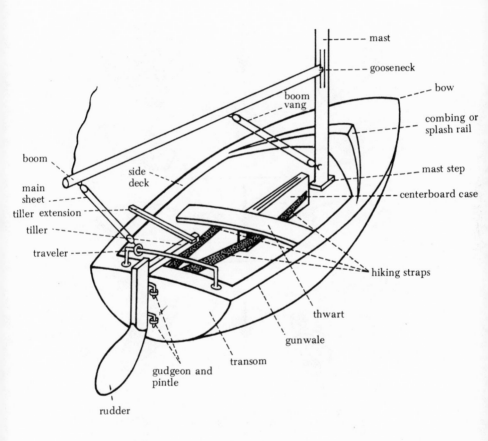

Appendix 5
Courses in Relation to the Wind

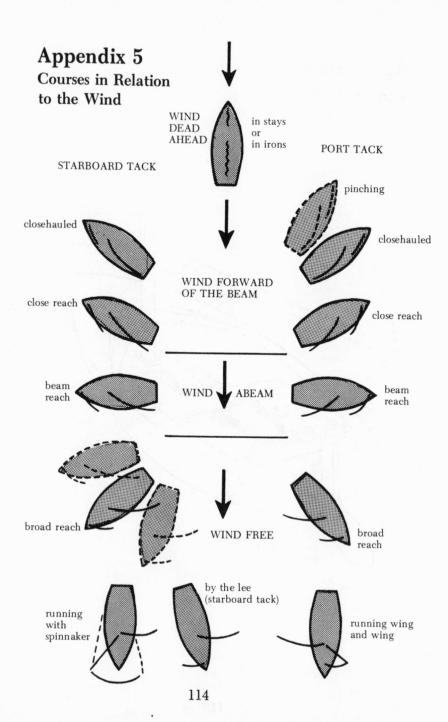

WIND DEAD AHEAD — in stays or in irons

STARBOARD TACK

PORT TACK

pinching

closehauled

closehauled

WIND FORWARD OF THE BEAM

close reach

close reach

beam reach

WIND ABEAM

beam reach

broad reach

WIND FREE

broad reach

running with spinnaker

by the lee (starboard tack)

running wing and wing

INDEX